Ask Albert Ellis

Ask Albert Ellis?

**Straight Answers and Sound Advice from
America's Best-Known Psychologist**

Albert Ellis, Ph.D.

Impact   Publishers®
ATASCADERO, CALIFORNIA

ATTENTION ORGANIZATIONS AND CORPORATIONS:
This book is available at quantity discounts on bulk purchases for educational,
business, or sales promotional use. For further information, please contact Impact
Publishers, P.O. Box 6016, Atascadero, CA 93423-6016, Phone: 1-800-246-7228, email:
sales@impactpublishers.com

Library of Congress Cataloging-in-Publication Data

Ellis, Albert.
    Ask Albert Ellis : straight answers and sound advice from America's
best known psychologist / Albert Ellis.
      p. cm.
    Includes bibliographical references and index.
    ISBN 1-886230-51-X (alk. paper)
      1. Rational-emotive psychotherapy--Miscellanea. 2. Ellis, Albert.
      I. Title.

RC489.R3E425 2003
616.89'14--dc21

                    2003047766

Publisher's Note
*This publication is designed to provide accurate and authoritative information in regard
to the subject matter covered. It is sold with the understanding that the publisher is not
engaged in rendering psychological, legal, financial, or other professional services. If
expert assistance or counseling is needed, the services of a competent professional
should be sought.*

Impact Publishers and colophon are registered trademarks of Impact Publishers, Inc.

Cover design by K.A. White Design, San Luis Obispo, California
Printed in the United States of America on acid-free paper.
Published by **Impact 🕊 Publishers®**
POST OFFICE BOX 6016
ATASCADERO, CALIFORNIA 93423-6016
www.impactpublishers.com

Dedication

To Debbie Joffe, who was enormously helpful in putting together this book and to the many people who sent me the questions that I answered in the book. Many Thanks!

Contents

Foreword

It is remotely possible that some readers of this book are wondering, "Who is Albert Ellis?" and/or "What is REBT?" This brief forward will introduce both, and will give you a quick overview of the treat that awaits you in the pages that follow.

Simply put, Dr. Albert Ellis is the most well-known and widely respected psychologist of our time. A practicing clinical psychologist for more than half a century, Dr. Ellis is President of the Albert Ellis Institute for Rational Emotive Behavior Therapy in New York City. He is author of *A New Guide to Rational Living; How to Make Yourself Happy; Feeling Better, Getting Better, Staying Better* and more than sixty other books, published in more than a dozen languages. His Rational Emotive Behavior Therapy method — REBT — was the first incarnation of today's most popular and proven psychotherapy approach — Cognitive Behavior Therapy — used by tens of thousands of therapists around the world,

Ask Albert Ellis is arguably his most "reader friendly" work. In this book, Albert Ellis responds to reader questions submitted to the very popular "Ask Dr. Ellis" website. His answers present the most straightforward, wide-ranging description yet of REBT.

Anyone who is seeking help in dealing with anxiety, depression, anger, or relationships, or who wants simply to understand more about REBT, will benefit from the sixty years of psychotherapy experience and wisdom about healthy thinking, healthy emotions, and healthy behavior which are distilled in this volume.

Ask Albert Ellis is divided into three sections. The first offers a very brief **Introduction** to REBT. Next come more than forty questions and answers about applying REBT concepts to **living a rational and healthy life**. Finally, some forty additional questions and answers are addressed to **professionals who do REBT** in their practice of psychotherapy, social work, classroom teaching, and more.

> Robert E Alberti, Ph.D.
> *Editor*

◆ ◆ ◆

Acknowledgements

I gratefully acknowledge the fine assistance of Patrice Ward and Tim Runion, who slaved over hot work-processors to put together the manuscript of this book and to Ariana Ruiz, who also helped greatly in getting the book out. As ever, Bob Alberti did some remarkably good editing and finished off my answers in very readable form.

Ask Albert Ellis...
"About
Rational Emotive
Behavior Therapy"
(REBT)

March 2002

Q *You're known worldwide as the "father" of Rational Emotive Behavior Therapy (REBT). What is REBT, and how does it differ from other therapies?*

♦

A First, you have to understand that what troubles us in life is not what happens to us, but how we *react* to what happens. The first-century philosopher Epictetus put it this way: "What disturbs people's minds is not events, but their judgments on events."

It's a pretty simple idea. You can make a situation better — or worse — by how you *think* about it, *feel* about it, and *behave* toward it. REBT is a powerful psychotherapy method that works because it helps people deal with the difficulties in their lives by changing the way they respond — think, feel, and behave —toward those difficulties.

Here's a simple example: Fred has worked for the Acme Widget Company for fifteen years. He has always received excellent reviews of his work performance. When Jane was hired as his assistant, Fred was asked to train her. He did, and now Jane has been promoted to a management job that Fred wanted. He is furious, believing he deserved the job. "This is *awful, terrible!*" Fred told his wife. "I *can't stand it!* That youngster comes in and jumps over me into the job I *should* have had! It isn't fair! Management is *horrible* for doing this!" And on, and on. Fred is *making himself* angry and depressed about a situation that he cannot control. It's true that this is *very disappointing* for Fred. And yes, it may not be fair (though we can't know all the details). But these things do happen, and we can choose to upset ourselves about them by believing they are *absolutely terrible,* or we can allow ourselves to be *disappointed and moderately upset,* but know that life will go on.

REBT is proven to help people deal with the difficulties in their lives by changing their thoughts, feelings, and behavior in response to events such as these, and to the way they respond — think, feel, and behave — toward the adversity.

Don't misunderstand, however. REBT does not say, "Roll over and accept whatever happens to you." REBT teaches you to *change what you can,* but to recognize that ranting and raving about things you can't change is *irrational* — that is, dysfunctional — and likely to make you needlessly disturbed.

◆ ◆ ◆

Q *There are lots of approaches to psychotherapy. How is REBT different?*

◆

A REBT is the original Cognitive Behavioral Therapy, and the first major therapy to recognize that people have *choices* about how they respond to life events — that everything is not dictated by the past. People do not really get disturbed by their early childhood and things that happen to them later, but they mainly disturb themselves - and they can *choose* to disturb themselves about these things or not.

I created REBT — which I then called Rational Emotive Therapy (RET) — in 1955, after I'd abandoned Rogerian therapy and psychoanalysis. Both methods were popular at that time, and I was trained in both, but found them too passive; neither approach emphasized what people could *do* about their disturbances, and neither prescribed homework assignments, which I considered important then and now.

When adversities happen to people, they can choose to make themselves either (1) *healthfully* negative — sorry and regretful and annoyed and frustrated and disappointed about the happening — or (2) *unhealthfully* negative — creating feelings of horror, terror, anxiety, depression, rage, and other disturbed feelings, along with dysfunctional behaviors. And even if they create these dysfunctional feelings and behaviors, they're able — because we humans are born *constructivists* — to reconstruct and to change them to healthy negative feelings and healthy negative behaviors, instead of unhealthy ones.

Rational Emotive Behavior Therapy offers a simple "ABC" structure to help explain how this works. Point "A" is an adverse event — such as failure or rejection by significant others. Point "B" represents the person's belief system or philosophy or view of what happens at "A." This view can be *rational* and *irrational*. Point "C" is the consequences the person creates as a result of "A" and "B."

Thus, if people rationally tell themselves, "I don't like 'A,' and I wish it were not so," then they feel healthfully sorry, disappointed, regretful about "A." On the other hand, if at point "B" they tell themselves — irrationally and unhealthfully — "It *shouldn't* be that bad. I *should* have made it better. Other people *shouldn't* have created this adversity for me. The world *shouldn't* have such events. It's *awful, terrible,* and *horrible,* and I *can't stand it.* I can't be happy *at all!*" Then — at point "C" — the consequences they produce are unhealthy negative feelings and unhealthy behaviors, such as obsessive-compulsiveness, drinking, running away, phobias, etc.

REBT is almost the first major form of therapy to use *thinking* and *emotional* and *behavioral* methods to dispute and minimize the irrational beliefs and turn them into rational preferences, which result in much healthier consequences at "C." So REBT has maybe thirty or forty cognitive (thinking) techniques, and just as many emotive techniques, and another set of behavioral techniques, just as many.

I showed, in my original paper on RET (REBT) at the American Psychological Association meeting in Chicago in 1956, that when humans *think* they also *feel* and *behave*. When they feel, they think and behave, and when they behave, they think and they feel. Therefore, to change their dysfunctional thoughts and feelings and behaviors, they had better use several cognitive, emotive, and behavioral techniques, and also use them interactionally.

Thus when they look at their nutty ideas at point "B" — "I have to do perfectly well and win the approval of significant others or else I am no good, or acting badly" — they have to *strongly* work at that nutty idea and *strongly* take action against it until they minimize it or get rid of it completely. Usually they just minimize it because they're born with the tendency to think rationally *and* irrationally.

Most of what people learn from their parents, their teachers, their cultures, the movies, etc., leaves them unable (or little able) to distinguish their rational from their irrational reactions without the help of therapy. Some do it by themselves, but they don't do it too well; with therapy they're helped to create an effective new philosophy: "I wish to hell I would do well and be loved by significant others, but, but, but I never *have to*. Now let's see what I can do to change the adversity at 'A.' If I *can* change it, fine, but if I can't, then I could live with it and still be a reasonably happy human."

It's that idea — learning to adopt a rational approach to dealing with life's inevitable adversities — that is the core of REBT.

◆ ◆ ◆

Q * *Is it really possible to change a long-standing disturbance in a few sessions of REBT?*

◆

A It's very possible to understand what people do to create disturbances in their lives, or to get them from their families, friends and community. They may have hated their parents or brothers or sisters for many years — telling themselves that family members should not act the way they do — and then they realize that they're doing this and they change. They didn't hate the others just because they acted badly, but because they had a command, a *Jehovian* command, that others *must not* act the way they do. And then they find that they can change that and start accepting their mother and father or sister and brother.

Usually it takes awhile to change a disturbing behavioral issue, such as being phobic about elevators or planes or trains. It takes awhile to act against it, *act against* it, *act against* it, and habituate themselves to the new philosophy: "Well, elevators and planes may have some danger attached to them, and may be very uncomfortable, but I can risk it and take this danger and get to the point where I am even comfortable and enjoy taking them."

◆ ◆ ◆

January 2001

Q *I have some doubts about our ability to change ourselves simply by reading books and other written material on the specific problem. Can you please give us your view on the likelihood of changing a behavior through cognitive processes such as reading and analysis?*

♦

A You are right in having some doubts about our ability to change ourselves by *merely* reading books and other material on our specific problems. Changing a behavior through *pure* cognitive processes is rarely, if ever, accomplished. As Rational Emotive Behavior Therapy (REBT) has shown since I created it in 1955, thinking, feeling, and behaving processes are virtually never "pure," but invariably importantly interact with and affect each other. Thus, when you have a dysfunctional behavior — such as a phobia against riding in elevators — you *think* that elevators are "very dangerous," when of course they are remarkably safe. You hold your mistaken belief very *strongly* and *emotionally*. And you consistently *act* on your thought and feeling by panicking yourself about the possibility of taking an elevator ride or even by contemplating taking one. You therefore, fearfully *avoid* elevators.

Obviously, your phobia has definite cognitive, emotional, and behavioral elements. So REBT, from the start, has shown people how to work at changing *all three* of these factors when they disturb themselves. It uses many philosophic *and* evocative-experiential *and* behavioral methods of psychotherapy — and that is why it is called Rational Emotive Behavior Therapy. Similarly, most other Cognitive Behavior therapies, which largely follow the practices of REBT, are "multimodal" — as psychologist Arnold Lazarus has advocated in his book, *Multi-Modal Therapy* — and use a number of interrelated active-directive techniques.

Self-help books and audio-visual materials that teach people REBT methods have been found to be quite effective when used in conjunction with live sessions of therapy — as several research studies have shown. This is because good materials of this kind are not merely *read* or *listened to* by people with problems, but because they show these people how to use thinking, feeling, and behavioral *homework assignments* to change themselves. Thus, David Burns' *Feeling Good*, my own *Guide to Rational Living*, and Alberti & Emmons' *Your Perfect Right* have significantly helped thousands of readers who actively and forcefully *apply* the techniques in these books. Throughout history, untold numbers of people have significantly helped themselves by sermons, talks, workshops, articles, and books — including, especially, that most read of all self-help books, *The Bible*. Individuals who suffer from mental and behavioral problems had often better have individual or group psychotherapy. But they can also considerably help themselves by effective writings and audio-visual materials. Yes, if they forcefully *work* at using some of the cognitive, experiential and behavioral methods that these materials urge them to apply.

◆　◆　◆

Q * *What are the "thinking" techniques that you recommend to help us become less disturbable?*

◆

A In my book, *Feeling Better, Getting Better, Staying Better,* I have a number of thinking techniques. The main one is to keep actively and strongly disputing your irrational beliefs. Again, if you think that you are no good when you screw up in front of people and they reject you, you say "prove" to yourself; "prove it's awful or terrible when I screw up. Where is it written that I *have to* do well? Logically how does it follow that if I screw up, I *am* a screw up who will put myself down in the present and future and who can never be loveable or acceptable by others? And where is it written that because I like *very, very* much to do well, I have to, and where will it get me if I keep telling myself I have to absolutely do well and be loved by others under all conditions, and it's terrible, terrible, awful, horrible and I'm no good if I don't?" And by asking these questions and looking for the real answers, the answers that you, yourself, could give, you'll see that there are no reasons why you absolutely *must* perform adequately, that it doesn't follow that you *are* no good when you *do* certain things badly, and it will keep getting you into trouble if you believe those irrational and other irrational beliefs and keep thinking about them.

◆ ◆ ◆

Q *What are some of the "feeling" techniques you recommend to help us become less disturbable?*

◆

A Well, there are several. One you very *strongly* tell yourself coping rational statements, such as the statement "I don't like failing and being rejected, but, but, but I can take it and live with it and still learn from it and be happy." And you put away your nutty ideas, such as the idea that you must win this person's — and only this person's — love forever. And you strongly dispute it and you let your friends and relatives listen to you disputing it, and tell you how to do it much more strongly and better.

Then you can do Rational Emotive Imagery — invented by Maxie Maultsby, Jr. — where you think of the worst thing happening, such as losing a very good job and not being able to get as good a one. You imagine that has really occurred; you let yourself feel exceptionally horrified or anxious or depressed about it. And then you work on changing your feelings so that you feel very sorry and disappointed about *it*, but you don't put yourself down about *you* for having failed.

REBT also teaches clients to unconditionally accept themselves no matter *what* they do. They don't like, again, *it*, but they accept themselves *with* it, and at the same time learn to unconditionally accept other people, no matter what they do. So even when the people act very *badly*, as evil as they could be in their actions, they don't see them as rotten, totally evil people, just as people who *acted* very, very badly *this time*, and are powerful humans and could change.

*Adapted from an interview with Albert Ellis, March 2002

Ask Albert Ellis...
"About
Living a More Rational
and Healthy Life"

Answers for the Rest of Us.

December 2002

Q *How does REBT distinguish between a person and her behavior? Is it legitimate to label a person as say, "good"?*

◆

A Your question is a good one, but it's not as easy to answer as you might think. Stay with me as I give you some background.

Rational Emotive Behavior Therapy (REBT) holds that although a person *does* her behavior, she is not what she *does*. This was brilliantly pointed out in 1933 by Alfred Korzybski, in his book, *Science and Sanity,* and was also shown by Bertrand Russell, Wilfred Quine, and several other philosophers. If you say to yourself, "I do well, therefore I *am* a *good person*," or if you say, "I perform poorly, therefore I *am* a *bad person,"* you make inaccurate *overgeneralizations*. If you were really a *good person,* you would *only* and *always* perform well; and, likewise, if you were really a *bad person,* you would always and only perform badly. But, of course, you are a *changeable* person, who *sometimes* acts well and *sometimes* behaves badly. What is more, you can *change* your inadequate and immoral behavior to adequate and moral behavior — and vice versa! Also, being human, you are inevitably *fallible,* never *absolutely perfect*. So you have very little chance of *always* performing well and *always* winning the approval of others. If you did so, it would be a miracle!

REBT considers it fairly illegitimate to label a person as "good"; that would be, as Korzybski pointed out, an overgeneralization. REBT joins Korzybski and the

International Society of General Semantics (which he founded), in opposing that kind of inaccurate labeling of people. But the existential philosophy of Martin Heidigger, Jean Paul Sartre, and Paul Tillich, allows you to cautiously — very cautiously! — say to yourself and believe, "I am a good person because I exist (am alive), I am human, and I am a unique individual." REBT allows you to take this "inelegant" solution to the problem of giving yourself worth as a person, because it is a *safe* solution.

If you believe that you are a "good person" because of your existence, your humanity, and individual uniqueness you can't lose — because, as long as you live, you will be alive, human, and unique. (So will all other people!) You can therefore have what REBT calls *unconditional self-acceptance* (USA) and *unconditional other-acceptance* (UOA). Consequently, you will never damn yourself (by labeling your*self* or *being* as "bad" or "no good") and you will never damn other *persons* as "bad" or "no good." You will adopt the Christian philosophy, "I accept the *sinner* but not the sin." That philosophy will help you be "good" even when you act "badly," and to see others as "good" even when they perform badly. That *view* of your worth and others' worth *as persons* will work — even when you and they *do* poorly. Moreover, it will usually help you *function* better. For when you give yourself *conditional* self-acceptance (which is often peculiarly called "self-esteem"), you only accept your*self when* you perform well and are approved by significant others, and you likewise damn your*self* when you fail. This creates anxiety even when you succeed because you are ready to damn yourself if you fail in the future. So conditional self-acceptance or "self-esteem" may make you anxious (or depressed) and *interferes* with your performances.

Unconditional self-acceptance (USA) and unconditional other-acceptance (UOA) lead to good results, and you can have them by merely *deciding* to take an existential view of your and other people's "worth." You *choose* to be a "good person" *just* because you are alive, human, and unique. As I said above, pretty safe!

Unfortunately, this view of yourself and others as always being "good" people is arbitrary and definitional — there is no way of empirically falsifying it or validating it. *You* say and believe that you're "good," but anyone else is entitled to hold that just because you exist, are human, and unique, you are "neutral" or "bad." What, then, *are* you?

I originated the REBT "elegant" solution to this problem of assessing your worth in the 1960s and have taught it to many clients and to many readers of my writings and listeners to my lectures and audio and videotapes. My solution agrees with Korzybski that it really is not legitimate to rate or evaluate your *global* self at all, and it tells you how to stop doing this.

First, you continue to evaluate or measure most of your behaviors — your thoughts, feelings, and actions — according to your *goals* or *purposes* in life. Thus, you normally want to remain alive and be reasonably happy and free from distinct pain when you are (1) alone, (2) with other agreeable people, (3) with a few close and intimate people, (4) with a satisfying vocation or profession, (5) with suitable interests (such as art, music, science, sports), and (6) with enjoyable recreation (such as reading, television, athletics, and creative activities).

When you do fulfill these goals — which nearly all people have — you tell yourself, *that* is "good." I fulfilled my goals and wasn't blocked too much from doing so. Therefore, I'll rate or evaluate my thoughts, feelings, and actions that enabled me to do so as "good" — because I basically got what I wanted and didn't get what I don't want. Obviously *that* is "good."

Conversely, when you fail to achieve your goals and purposes, you tell yourself *that* is bad. I didn't get what I wanted or got what I didn't want. My desires are unfulfilled — and *that* is "bad."

Once you decide or choose what you desire and what you don't desire — which, as a live human, you are presumably entitled to and able to decide — then *only* rate or evaluate the *performances* — that helped you or hindered you. *They* are "desirable" or "undesirable" and therefore (to you) "good" or "bad." However! Do not rate or evaluate your *global self* or *being.* Don't *label* your entire *personhood* as "good" or "bad," because you then (inaccurately) *over*generalize. By the same token (still following Korzybski) do not label other *people*: their *self, being, essence,* or *soul. They* are not "good" or "bad." But, according to your preferences and desires (and the social standards of the community in which they live) their *behaviors* can be viewed as "good" or "bad."

The world in which you live has "good" events that aid your and your social community's goals and purposes; and it has "bad" events that interfere with these purposes. But it, the world itself, is not seen as being *globally* "good" or "bad," although it has many happenings, events, and problems that you may view as "okay," or "not okay," or as somewhere in between.

REBT favors your deciding on definite goals, purposes, and values — which you inevitably have to do in order to remain alive and reasonably satisfied with your life. But it tries to help you to refuse to make global, overgeneralized ratings of your*self* or *personhood,* of other people's *self* or *personhood,* and of the world and its whole *existence* or *essence.* If you work at *refusing to overgeneralize,* you will tend to stop damning or deifying yourself or anyone — and will only rate your and their *doings*. Try it!

◆ ◆ ◆

Q *How can we make ourselves happy?*

◆

A As you're working on your irrational beliefs and your dysfunctional behaviors — the consequence partly of these beliefs — you can then have the time and energy to ask yourself what do you as a unique individual really like to do and not like to do. You can then creatively find things that will make you actually happy, rather than just nondisturbed, and then go on to find a few things that may make you very, very happy — like love or sex or work or anything else. But each of us is an individual, and we can't tell anybody else how they can be happy. They can usually find it out for themselves if they stop upsetting themselves with their irrational beliefs and their dysfunctional behaviors.

◆ ◆ ◆

November 1997

Q *It is understandable that a victim of abuse or neglect might feel "less worthy" than others. Why, I keep wondering, is it that a great many people who have never been abused, and come from a well-adjusted environment, lack the necessary confidence to flourish in life and to find self-acceptance? This is particularly evident among women — women who are "successes" and have no apparent reason for feeling that they are "less worthy" individuals than* *someone else. It is almost as if women more frequently do not view themselves accurately. They are evaluating themselves to be lesser than the rest of society views them. If I am to help my sisters, I must better understand the sources of their low self-esteem and poor self-image.*

◆

Self-downing or lack of self-acceptance has biological as well as social sources. All humans have to rate or evaluate their behaviors in order to survive and fulfill their goals. But when they rate their thoughts, feelings, and deeds, they have an inborn tendency, which is exacerbated by their social learning, to overgeneralize and to globally rate themselves. Thus, when they behave well they inaccurately think, "I am a good person" and when they behave badly they unrealistically think, "I am a bad person." Because behaving badly can lead to dire results — including ostracism and death — they are more likely to say "I am a bad person" when they fail to do well than "I am a good person" when they succeed in doing well. For safety's sake, they wrongly believe, "I absolutely must do well and be approved by significant others" instead of "It is highly preferable that I perform well and be approved but it is not absolutely necessary." Consequently, when they behave inefficiently they tend to put themselves down rather than merely criticize and correct their behavior. Their social learning frequently encourages them to do this kind of self-downing. In our culture, it encourages women to have higher goals and values — that is, to be "nicer" and "more attractive" than men — and thereby fosters more self-criticism and self-downing. Women, and men too, would be less prone to feeling "less worthy" if they were shown, as Rational Emotive Behavior Therapy (REBT) teaches them, to unconditionally accept themselves whether or not they performed well and whether or not they were universally approved. All humans are exceptionally fallible and unconditional self-acceptance (USA) helps them acknowledge their fallibility and still not put themselves down for it.

◆ ◆ ◆

Q *You suggest in your book,* How to Make Yourself Happy, *that there are "action ways to make yourself less disturbable." Would you comment on some of them please?*

◆

A Let's suppose you *think* it's terrible to be rejected by somebody you really are attracted to, and therefore you're shy and powerless to do something about it. When you start working on that belief cognitively, but very strongly, you tell yourself that it's *inconvenient* and *sad* and *unfortunate* if a person you really like doesn't like you, but it should be the way it is and it's not terrible, because terrible means it's almost *more* than bad. Yes, it may be *very, very* bad to you, but it shouldn't be *so* bad that it's terrible and you can't stand it or be happy at all.

What to do? Very forcefully many times *contradict* that belief. You have to force yourself into action in order to really get rid of a belief. Take the risk, do what I call "shame-attacking" exercises — foolishly say things or do things in front of that person — and see that you don't *feel* ashamed; you just feel sorry and regretful, and take the risk of being rejected, get rejected many times, and see that the world doesn't come to an end.

The same thing with phobia or severe avoidance. If you're afraid of elevators or trains, or people because they might reject you, and therefore you avoid them at all costs, you'd better minimize your idea that something *terrible* will happen if you don't avoid them. You very likely will fail again and be rejected, but you won't be a "no-goodnik" for failing and being rejected, so you better dispute that idea actively as well. Force yourself *uncomfortably* to approach people that you're afraid of, or *uncomfortably* go in the elevator, or the train or the airplane and see that nothing terrible happens. Only by doing the uncomfortable thing will you'll see that it's not fatal or very, very horrible.

REBT always includes a combination of *thinking* techniques and *feeling* techniques and *behavioral* techniques. And doing my shame-attacking exercises you deliberately do something silly, foolish and rejectable in public, such as tell somebody that you just got out of the mental hospital, or yell the stops in the subway trains so people think you're crazy. And you deliberately do that thing in order to work on believing that, "When people think I'm crazy and put me down, I never have to agree with them and put myself down." As Eleanor Roosevelt said, "Nobody can insult you without your permission."

"Though it's true and I regret the fact that they don't like me, I can still accept myself unconditionally." So REBT especially teaches unconditional acceptance — *whether or not* you do well, and whether significant people love you — and gets you to take risks, actual behavioral risks, to prove that you can accept yourself even if others do not.

◆ ◆ ◆

March 2001

Q *What are the ten irrational beliefs that people have?*

◆

People have more than ten irrational or dysfunctional beliefs — in fact, they may have scores of them. Just about all of these beliefs, however, can be put under three main headings:

1. I *absolutely must* perform important functions well and be approved by significant people for doing so. If not, I am a pretty worthless individual.
2. Other people *absolutely must* treat me kindly and fairly, or else they are damnable persons.
3. The conditions under which I live *absolutely should* be nice, easy, and enjoyable. Else I cannot enjoy life at all.

In my best-selling book, *A Guide to Rational Living*, I describe ten related irrational beliefs and show how to make them more rational and functional. These are:

1. The idea that you must — yes, must — have love or approval from all the significant people in your life.
2. The idea that you absolutely must be thoroughly competent, adequate, and achieving.
3. The idea that people absolutely must not act obnoxiously and unfairly, and that when they do, you should blame and damn them, and see them as bad, wicked, or rotten individuals.
4. The idea that you have to see things as being awful, terrible, horrible, and catastrophic when you are seriously frustrated or treated unfairly.
5. The idea you must be miserable when you have pressures and difficult experiences; and that you have little ability to control, and cannot change, your disturbed feelings.
6. The idea that if something is dangerous or fearsome, you must obsess about it and frantically try to escape from it.

7. The idea that you can easily avoid facing many difficulties and self-responsibilities and still lead a highly fulfilling existence.
8. The idea that your past remains all-important and that because something once strongly influenced your life, it has to keep determining your behaviors and feelings today.
9. The idea that people and things absolutely must be better than they are and that it is awful and horrible if you cannot change life's grim facts to suit you.
10. The idea that you can achieve maximum human happiness by inertia and inaction or by passively and uncommittedly "enjoying yourself."

◆ ◆ ◆

January 2000

It's easy for me to find an irrational belief and to dispute against it only when it's NOT my problem. When it comes to my own problem, I cannot be cool enough to think about it rationally. I always try, but I fail. My emotion is out of control and I'm so overwhelmed. How can I stay cool to deal with my own problem?

◆

It is difficult for many people to find their irrational beliefs and dispute them for several reasons, including these:

1. They are very upset, as you are, and have great difficulty disputing irrational beliefs when they are so upset. Therefore, they had better use a relaxation technique, such as Herbert Benson's Relaxation Response or Edmund Jacobson's Progressive

Relaxation Technique, to *first* calm themselves. *Then* their overwhelming emotion will not interfere with their disputing.

2. They *think* they are too upset to dispute their irrational beliefs and demand that they not be upset. Then they make themselves *doubly* upset and all progress stops.

3. They find it difficult to dispute their irrational beliefs, incorrectly telling themselves that it is *too* difficult to do so. Therefore they give up trying. They *easily* think irrationally and think it should be *easy* to change once they *recognize* that they do so. Actually, it is often hard to do so and they refuse to *persist* at the disputing.

4. They blame themselves for not quickly and easily disputing their irrational beliefs. This secondary self-damning itself is irrational and makes them *more* disturbed. They then focus on their self-damning so intently that they can hardly think of anything else, including the disputing of their original and their secondary irrational beliefs.

Look for these blocks to strongly and persistently disputing your irrational beliefs. Allow yourself some time to relax and then to discover and dispute the above kinds of irrational beliefs that may interfere with your disputing.

◆ ◆ ◆

April 1998

Q *Isn't it true that some irrational/unprovable beliefs can have a healthy effect on an individual? (e.g., My relationship with my wife is Fabulous!) If so, is it really accurate to pin psychological distress on having irrational, unprovable beliefs? Wouldn't it be more helpful just to say that we have "choices" in how we can view a situation, figure out which choice will serve our long-term interests the best, and then pick it, rather than worry about whether a belief is rational or irrational?*

◆

A In Rational Emotive Behavior Therapy (REBT), irrational beliefs are not merely defined as those that are unrealistic (anti-factual) or illogical (do not follow from one's premises), but include those that are usually unrealistic and illogical *and also* do harm to you and/or your social group (sabotage your goals and desires). If you believe that your wife is Fabulous when she is actually fairly ordinary, that is unrealistic. If you believe that because you love her, that makes her Fabulous to everyone, that is unrealistic and illogical. But these unrealistic and illogical beliefs are *healthy* in that they help both you and your wife and presumably do not harm anyone else. Therefore, in REBT theory and practice they are *not irrational.* You are both damned lucky! If you believe that because you love her and because you see her as Fabulous she will never make any mistakes nor treat you unkindly, beware! That is probably *unrealistic, illogical* and *self-defeating!*

◆ ◆ ◆

August 1996

Q *Would anyone who has no self-destructive beliefs be happy for their whole life even if their surroundings are very negatively colored?*

◆

A No, a person with no self-destructive beliefs — which would be rare! — would not be *needlessly* anxious, depressed, enraged, or self-downing. But he or she would often be quite sorry, sad, disappointed, and frustrated about unfortunate life events. These are hardly happy feelings! But they help the person cope healthily with negative events, try to change them, and look for as much happiness as she or he can find in spite of adversities. Rational Emotive Behavior Therapy (REBT) shows people how to ward off panic and depression, to still feel sorrow and regret when negative events occur, and to find some kind of enjoyment even when life is very negatively colored.

◆ ◆ ◆

Q *Can we really change ourselves when we have self-defeating behaviors?*

◆

A Yes, if we work very hard at it. We're prone biologically to think and feel and behave badly at times against our own interests and against the social interest of our culture and community. And then we learn these behaviors as well. It's fairly easy using REBT to see what we're doing, but it takes quite a lot of effort and often a period of time to change what we think — and thus how we act.

◆ ◆ ◆

August 2002:

Q *Why do so many therapies and world views often take an orientation to the past rather than a commitment to the future? A recent conversation illustrates. To a friend I conveyed a quote from a Buddhist teacher that inspired me: "The only thing I own are my actions." To which she replied, "I don't even know if we own our actions." I am heartened by REBT's and other forward-looking approaches; but why do we cling to the past when we examine our lives? Is it simply that it is too much work to take responsibility for our actions?*

◆

A We probably cling to the past when we examine our lives for several reasons:

1. It seems logical for us to assume that because the past, along with our *views* of it, did once affect us, it always will.
2. We are prone, as humans, to believe that *events* contributed to our disturbance in the past, and that by themselves *made* us disturbed.
3. Several important theories of disturbance, such as psychoanalysis, and behavioral conditioning, strongly — and somewhat inaccurately — convince us of the crucial importance of the past.
4. We *like* to believe that external events, including past ones, caused us to be upset, rather than take partial responsibility for creating our upsetness *ourselves*. So believing this to be true is something of a copout.
5. We *prefer* to believe that past events upset us and that merely understanding how they did so will easily and automatically get us to change. This kind of insight has its advantages, but we still have to modify our *present* thoughts, feelings, and behaviors in order to effectively change.

Yes, your friend seems correct. We do not *completely* know if we own our actions. We *partly* and *importantly* have some significant choices of our actions; but we are inevitably restricted by biological and social learning influences that limit our choices. Therefore, if we clearly see and change our dysfunctional thinking, feeling, and behaving, as Rational Emotive Behavior Therapy shows us how to do, we can take forward-looking steps to considerably improve our present and future. Yes, we often may refuse to take responsibility for our actions. But we can!

◆ ◆ ◆

June 2000

What role do you think the environment plays in our emotions? Would all environments be equally conducive to happiness if we were able to completely master our thinking?

◆

The environment usually plays a large part in our emotions because it presents us with many *Activating Events* (A's): some that we like or prefer and many that we dislike or do not prefer. We usually feel good or happy about preferable A's and feel bad or unhappy about disliked A's. When we *Believe* (at point B) that preferable A's absolutely *must exist* when they actually do not, or that unpreferable A's absolutely *must not exist* when they actually do, we make ourselves anxious, depressed, or enraged at point C (*Consequence*). If we completely mastered our absolutistic thinking — which is highly unlikely — when we encountered bad environmental conditions at point A, we would rarely feel very emotionally disturbed at point C, but we would still feel healthfully upset (sorry or regretful). The theory of REBT says that A (Activating Events or environmental conditions) times B (Beliefs) equals C (consequences), or AxB=C so the environment is a key point in this equation. If our environment (A) was unusually good, but we absolutistically Believed (B) that it *must* be even better, we would still suffer with anxiety or depression (C). What we call emotional disturbance (C) usually follows from *both* A (events in the environment) and B (dysfunctional Beliefs about the environment).

◆ ◆ ◆

July 1997

Q *I know that we can use our wills to direct our actions, but are our wills really free? Are we completely governed by our heredity and environment, which are both beyond our control? On what other factors besides heredity and environment could a decision be based?*

◆

A No, our wills are not completely free, nor are we completely governed by our heredity and environment. We seem to be born and reared with some degree of choice, agency, or self-control, but have to work at accepting its limitations and push ourselves to use it adequately. As I note in my book, *Better, Deeper, and More Enduring Brief Therapy,* what I call "will power" consists of several steps, including:

1. Deciding to change thoughts, feelings, and behaviors.
2. Acquiring the knowledge of how to change them.
3. Determining to back up your decision and use your knowledge.

4. Forcefully acting on your decision, your knowledge and determination.
5. Continuing many times to maintain your decision and determination, and using your knowledge and acting on it.
6. Refusing to damn yourself when you have will but little will power.
7. Continuing the work and practice of acting on your will to achieve will power

◆ ◆ ◆

May 2002

Q *I am interested in finding out about the REBT method of dealing with someone (that would be me) who has either a fear of success or a lack of drive.*

◆

A The REBT method of dealing with people who have a fear of success is, first, to find out whether they *really* fear succeeding. Very few people actually do. Behind their "fear of success," they usually have a fear of *failing* in some way. Thus, they may, because they succeed at certain tasks, *fail* to *keep* succeeding; *fail* to succeed *well enough*; *fail* to please others who are jealous of their success, etc. So, they really fear some "horrible" *consequence* of succeeding. REBT shows them that, yes, there are often unfortunate consequences of success, but that these are merely *inconveniences* and not "great dangers" or "horrors." Usually, the hassles that go with succeeding are mild — and are well worth it!

Lack of drive may have biological causes, which can be ascertained and either remedied or, if unremedied, can be accepted without self-damning. In most cases, it results when people create lack of motivation by convincing themselves that pushing themselves is "too hard"; that it *must not* be as hard as it is; and that it's "awful" for them to have to work so hard to get the results they would like to get *easily*. So they have low frustration tolerance — which we commonly call "laziness."

In addition, people with lack of drive very frequently also have, as I mentioned above, "fear of success" underlain by "fear of failure." They tell themselves that they *absolutely must* succeed at important projects or at winning approval, and that if they fail they are *worthless people*. They thereby make it too "risky" to even try to motivate themselves to succeed. So they cop out and sit on their rumps. Then they castigate themselves for being unmotivated!

REBT uses many thinking, feeling, and behavioral methods to help people who suffer from low frustration tolerance, such as those described in my book with William Knaus, *Overcoming Procrastination*. It also has many techniques of helping people overcome their strong tendencies to hate themselves when they take the healthy risks of failing and of being rejected by others. These multimodal methods of dealing with failure and rejection are described in several of my books, especially, *A Guide to Rational Living*, and *Feeling Better, Getting Better, Staying Better*.

Motivating yourself to drive for success and for approval has distinct inconveniences and hazards, but life without any risk-taking would be incredibly boring!

◆ ◆ ◆

December 1997

Q *Understanding that to accomplish some things you often need to force yourself to do them if you want to get them done. How do you actually force yourself? From experience, not so easily.*

◆

A You force yourself by first giving up the irrational, self-defeating belief that because you want them to be done easily, without effort, there should be an easy, magical way to do things. Then you accept, without necessarily liking, several grim facts of life:
  1. Things won't do themselves — not very often!
  2. You'll benefit by doing them and do yourself in by procrastinating.
  3. It's often hard, but not *too hard,* to do them.
  4. If things are hard to do, that's the way they should be — hard.
  5. As Benjamin Franklin said, "There are no gains without pains."
  6. There's one main way to accomplish things — PYA (Push Your Ass).
  7. If you don't, you're not an idiot, but you have acted idiotically this time!
  8. It's hard to change, but it's much harder if you don't.

◆ ◆ ◆

April 1999

Q *How important do you feel it is to have goals for achievement, sense of direction and mental health?*

◆

A Goal setting is an important, and even an essential, part of life. Our main goal is to survive and to be happy in various ways, including personal achievement, mental health, and good relations with other people. When we don't seem to have goals, we usually do have them in our underlying desires, but we sometimes insist that we *absolutely must* achieve them and achieve them remarkably well. Our demand that we *have to* achieve our goals then leads to anxiety in case we don't accomplish them remarkably well. Consequently, we make achieving them too "dangerous," and often cop out and make ourselves goal-less.

If we give up our grandiose *demands* that our goals *must* be achieved, but still keep our strong *desire* to attain them, we usually have several possible goals — and can choose to work on those we prefer over our other goals. Many goals — such as saving money and spending it on other goals — are contradictory. Too bad! — but we can't have everything. So if we keep our goals and desires, but refuse to make them *absolute necessities*, we can work things out, make compromises, and achieve many of the things we want much — but hardly all — of the time.

◆ ◆ ◆

June 2002

Q *While discussing the basic tenets of REBT with a friend recently, he suggested that adjusting one's way of thinking about his or her problems in life encourages one to "settle," and not to attempt to change one's situation or circumstances. What would you respond to the charge that*

REBT teaches one to settle for whatever happens, thereby discouraging action?

◆

REBT definitely does not encourage people to "settle" and fail to change one's situation or circumstances. As recommended by theologian Reinhold Niebuhr in the famous Serenity Prayer adopted by Alcoholics Anonymous, it encourages people to try very hard to change unfortunate and obnoxious conditions that they *can* change. Otherwise, there will be no progress for themselves or the community in which they live. Their goals are to gain human happiness for themselves and members of their social group. These goals often require exceptionally hard work. REBT distinctly favors *work and practice* for self-development *and* community growth. It fosters productivity and change.

When they are faced with hassles and troubles, people can use REBT to feel the *healthy* negative emotions of sorrow and disappointment, which can motivate them to review their difficulties, instead of feeling the *unhealthy* negative emotions of panic, depression, and rage, which will help immobilize them. REBT shows them how to have strong healthy rather than unhealthy feelings when they are faced with adversities. This, again, requires them to *work* at achieving healthy, forward-pushing emotions.

Once people feel frustrated but not panicked about unfortunate happenings, they then can use many problem-solving methods that Rational Emotive Behavior Therapy employs. For example, after minimizing the upsetness, they can figure out solutions to environmental and other difficulties; obtain relevant information to help solve their problems; use cost-benefit analysis to discover what solutions are best; experimentally try alternate plans, to see which bring better results; and push, push, push in several other ways to change themselves and their external environment.

REBT shows people how to fight their disturbances in an exceptionally active-directive manner, and thereby encourages them to determinedly try to change the world.

◆ ◆ ◆

July 1999

Q *REBT is famous for elegantly and rationally assessing underlying assumptions behind behaviors. But for purposes of decision-making, does this approach allow for the role of* intuition *when evidence is scanty or the motives of others unclear?*

◆

A REBT uses a special cognitive technique to help people make decisions. It is called *referenting* or *cost-benefit analysis.* For example, to make a decision as to which job to take, you make a list of all the benefits of taking it and rate each benefit from one to ten, in accordance with how you rate it and feel about it. You also make a list of all the disbenefits you will most likely receive from it and rate each disbenefit from one to ten, again in accordance with how you rate it and feel about it. Your ratings are partly intuitive — meaning, you guess at them and their outcome. So intuition or guess-work based on personal feelings is probably always included in decision-making.

Even when you make a decision in favor of one job or another (or about almost anything else) by doing a cost-benefit analysis, you make your final decision by intuition, in that you *guess* how you will feel and act after you make your decision. But you don't absolutely *know* what your thoughts, feelings, and actions are or will eventually be. Even when you decide that two and two equal four, you not only go by mathematical convention but also how you *feel* about this convention. So, yes, REBT allows you to use your intuition when evidence is scanty or the motives of others are unclear.

◆ ◆ ◆

December 2000

In your experience, can we ever really overcome our tendency to "this must be," "it would be awful if," and so forth? Are Irrational Beliefs "wired" into us? Or is REBT a bit like Zen, where we hope for brief periods of clarity and freedom, but spend a lot of time forgiving ourselves for falling short of our goal?

◆

No, we probably never really overcome our tendency to think, "Because I strongly desire to succeed at important tasks and to win the approval of significant others, I absolutely *must* do so, and I am a pretty *worthless person*, and it is *horrible* and *awful* if I fail and am rejected!" Our goals and desires to perform well, and to be approved by others for doing so, are probably both "wired in" and socially learned. Our tendency to unrealistically escalate our strong desires into absolutistic *musts* and *demands* (as I have said since 1955) are also both innate and learned. As humans, we not only generalize — which is fine — but we also frequently over generalize — which often is foolish and self-disturbing. Therefore, it is highly unlikely that we will ever completely conquer this human biosocial tendency.

However, when we inevitably fallible humans fall short of completely eliminating our absolutistic, inflexible *musts* and *demands,* and when we keep exaggeratingly *awfulizing* about our failings, rejections, and misfortunes, there are constructive steps we can take. We can use Rational Emotive Behavior Therapy, Cognitive Behavior Therapy, and other sensible philosophical and behavior change methods to do several things:

First, as you note, we can forgive ourselves for being fallible humans who often fail to achieve our goals. We are almost perfectly imperfect! But we can always give ourselves what the late psychologist Carl Rogers and I call Unconditional Self-acceptance (USA). Yes, just because we are alive and human, no other condition is required — unless we idiotically require it.

Second, we can give all other people — yes, all of them — unconditional other-acceptance (UOA). They, too, are incredibly fallible!

Third, we can work at acquiring Unconditional Life Acceptance (ULA), High Frustration Tolerance (HFT), or what I call "anti-awfulizing." That is, we can acknowledge that unfortunate events will often affect us (as the ancient Buddhists rightly said), but that they don't have to ruin our entire lives, that we can often be happy in spite of them. Providing that we stubbornly refuse to awfulize about them!

If we train ourselves to fairly consistently acquire USA, UOA, ULA, and HFT, we will still not *completely* eliminate our strong tendencies to *musturbate* and *awfulize.* But, with much cognitive, emotive, and behavioral hard work and practice, we can significantly and appreciably reduce them. Let us accept this challenge!

◆ ◆ ◆

May 2000

Q *My professor had the opportunity to train under you. He has mentioned in many of his lectures a term he said you used — awfulizing. I would appreciate a more comprehensive explanation of this term as I am not completely sure of its meaning.*

◆

A I invented the term *awfulizing* in the 1960s, after I first had invented the term *catastrophizing* in the 1950s. This is because I saw, when I originated Rational Emotive Behavior Therapy (REBT) at the beginning of 1955, that people often make "catastrophies" out of adversities and problems and blow unfortunate events out of proportion. Thus, if they fail to pass a test or succeed at a job interview, they feel and act as if utter disaster has occurred, and conclude that they will never pass a test or get a good job for the rest of their lives. They thereby "catastrophize" about important but still relatively minor failures and losses. I realized a little later, however, that real catastrophies sometimes do exist — such as prolonged child abuse, hurricanes, famines, earthquakes, floods, widespread terrorism, and wars. When these calamities actually occur, and people are shocked and depressed about them, they are hardly exaggeratedly catastrophizing. They are truly troubled and had better energetically strive to cope with them and prevent them in the future.

As I kept using REBT, and thereby helping people minimize their catastrophizing over relatively minor adversities, I saw that they also needlessly horrified themselves about many rejections and losses that were indeed unfortunate, but that they *additionally* called — or defined — as "awful" and "terrible." These happenings were realistically "bad" or "very bad" — because people failed to get something they prized or experienced troubles they abhorred. So that was, in their view, indeed unfortunate. By thinking of their misfortune as "awful" or "horrible," however, they raised it to an enormity — and, often, to a nonexistent "horror." For when they told themselves that it was "awful" for a loss or a failure to occur, they usually made it much *more* unfortunate than it actually was and thereby needlessly suffered greater frustration and misery than when they merely saw it as "bad." When anyone defines a misfortune as "awful," they frequently first mean that it is unfortunate or is even *very* unfortunate. That is their honest personal judgment or evaluation — and they are, of course, entitled to it because they are the deciders of how "good" or "bad" it is *for them.* But when they add that this same event is "terrible" or "awful" they often state or imply several mistaken, illogical, and self-defeating ideas:

1. The adversity they experience is "awful" because it is *totally* bad. (But, of course misfortunes are practically never *entirely* bad. They also have some advantages or good points. Awfulizing often arbitrarily *defines* them as *completely* bad.)

2. The adversity is as bad as it possibly could be. (But, actually, it just about always could be worse — and sometimes much worse — than it is.)

3. Because it is *so* bad, the adversity *absolutely must not* exist and be as bad as it is. (But, obviously, it has to be just as bad as it is. Its degree of badness doesn't prevent it from existing.)

4. It is *so* bad that the victims of this misfortune *absolutely cannot stand it.* (But in point of fact, no matter how much they dislike it, they *can* stand it and will rarely die of it.)

5. It is *so* bad that its victims cannot now be happy in any way — and must be completely miserable for the rest of their lives. (But, of course, they will only be completely miserable because they *think* they will be. Actually, they could still enjoy many pleasures if they *allowed* themselves to do so.)

In Rational Emotive Behavior Therapy, therapists fully acknowledge that their clients' adversities may indeed be unfortunate, and sometimes *very* unfortunate, and empathize with their clients about them. But they show these clients that such adversities had better not be defined or interpreted as "awful" and "horrible" because seeing them in that exaggerated light will make them seem much worse than they actually are and will escalate the clients' life problems into seemingly insurmountable "disasters." People will live with much less disturbance and considerably more happiness when, as theologian Reinhold Niebuhr said in the early 1900s, they change the adversities that they can change, when they accept (but not like) those they cannot change, and when they have wisdom to know the difference. They will then strongly *dislike* but rarely *awfulize* about the troubles and problems that unfortunately beset them.

◆ ◆ ◆

August 1998

Q *My daughter is nine years old and we are concerned about her moody character. My wife and I know that my daughter is suffering from some kind of depression but we don't know whom to ask for help. Today I decided to start searching over the Internet and I really need your advice. Please, what can we do?*

◆

A While I can't say from your brief question, your
daughter may indeed be suffering from some kind of
depression. This may be related to something she perceives
as too difficult to solve, or from blaming herself for her
shortcomings or lack of approval. She may possibly be
biologically inclined to dysthmia (mood swings) or
depression. I would recommend her being seen by a
Rational Emotive Behavior Therapist or a Cognitive
Behavior Therapist who treats children and also, possibly,
by a child psychiatrist who is not psychoanalytic. Read my
book, *A Guide to Rational Living*, to learn why many
children and adults are prone to anxiety and depression.

◆ ◆ ◆

April 2001

Q *My husband and I know from living Rational Emotive
Behavior Therapy that you are correct. When we started to
learn that our own expectations were causing us the
problem, and not the events in our lives, we saved our
marriage, and our lives. My question is in relation to my
fourteen-year-old daughter. She was sexually abused by her
biological father until the age of eight when we found out
and put him in jail. How do we begin to help her? How do
we recognize the false beliefs she may have developed as a
result?*

◆

A I am happy to know that (REBT) has helped you and
your husband so much with your lives and helped save
your marriage. You had better talk to your fourteen-year-old

daughter, or preferably have an REBT mental health professional talk to her with you, to try to see exactly what Irrational Beliefs she may have developed as a result of being sexually abused by her biological father.

She may have several self-helping Rational Beliefs, such as:

"It wasn't my fault that I was sexually abused.

"My father was probably very disturbed when he abused me and disturbed people frequently do immoral acts. But he was only a *person who* did bad acts and was not a completely *bad* person.

"People may wrongly put me down for being sexually abused, but I can live with their blaming and not take it too seriously.

"It's very *bad* that I was abused, but it's not *awful*, and I can lead a successful and happy life in spite of it.

"I'd better be cautious about having sex with anyone in the future, but not think that all men are disturbed and will try to abuse me."

Along with these self-helping and Rational Beliefs, your daughter — like many other sexually abused children — may have several harmful, Irrational Beliefs, such as:

"My father was a total scoundrel and a completely bad person.

"Coming from such bad stock, I may also be a rotten individual.

"Because my father sexually abused me, I am a soiled and terrible person.

"It's unfair that my father abused me and life must never be that unfair.

"I should have made my father stop abusing me and because I didn't I am an inadequate person.

"My mother should not have married and lived with a rotten man like my father, and she should have discovered his abuse of me immediately and got rid of him much sooner. Since she didn't, she's a weak and careless person!"

As can be seen from these possible examples, your daughter could have constructed a good many Rational (self-helping) and Irrational (self-defeating) Beliefs about being sexually abused by her father. Go with her to see an empathic Rational Emotive Behavior or Cognitive Behavior therapist, to help discover her main Rational and Irrational Beliefs. A good therapist will identify cognitive, emotive, and behavioral methods that can help her keep her rational dislikes and regrets about what happened to her and give up her irrational demands that bad things like sexual abuse absolutely *must not* occur and *must* lead her to damn others and herself when they do occur.

◆ ◆ ◆

October 2002

Q *Is forgiveness necessary for effective recovery from betrayal (from adultery, sexual abuse, etc)? Although clergy and some therapists would want us to strive toward forgiveness, it does not seem natural for everyone to do so. My alternative to forgiving (from a major betrayal) would be to "not forgive as a moral choice." What do you think?*

◆

A Forgiveness is a difficult issue and most people never quite resolve it because they do not see the difference between judging what their betrayers do as wrong or immoral and judging their betrayers as *bad people* when they do bad *acts*. When we damn the *doers* of immoral or unethical *behaviors* as "bastards" or "bitches," we say that they are responsible for their misdeeds, which may well be true; and we also say that they are evil *people*, which is invariably false. Because an *evil person* would always and forever commit only evil deeds, which not even was true of Adolf Hitler.

Condemning, first, a person's misdeed and, second, his or her entire *self* or *personhood*, usually leads to making ourselves angry, furious, enraged, revengeful, and vindictive. If we do it as a social group, community, or nation, and condemn other *groups* for their supposedly immoral *acts*, we produce feuds, wars, genocide, and holocausts. When we condemn the sinner, as well as his or her sins, we often create a high individual and social cost.

If you choose to be unforgiving, your feelings of revenge and vindictiveness that often accompany this choice are also costly to you, the unforgiver. They rip up your gut, subject you to psychosomatic ailments, help make your targets angrier and more likely to commit worse deeds, preoccupy your time and energy, and bring other dismal results. Does unforgiving help your betrayers acknowledge their destructive behavior and improve their ways in the future? Very rarely!

Is the answer given by my questioner, therefore, correct: to assess the wicked acts of your betrayer as bad acts and "not forgive as a moral choice"? Not so fast! You may justifiably assess his or her *betrayal* as irresponsible and immoral — since betrayal is hardly a good response to helping or trusting someone. But you had better not judge her or him to be a totally *irresponsible person*. This is an arrent overgeneralization, because it ignores all the good and proper deeds your betrayer has done (and will do) and sees the *betrayal* as the *whole* of him or her. This is certainly an inaccurate conclusion!

The answer that Rational Emotive Behavior Therapy gives to this frequent human problem is precise: Hold, and sometimes strongly hold forever, that in your considered opinion the betrayal was quite wrong, but still refuse to thoroughly damn the *personhood* of your betrayer. Stick to social reality — that the betrayal was against your interest and therefore was bad. But avoid overgeneralizing and musturbating *about* the betrayal. Stop idiotically telling yourself,

"My betrayal *absolutely should not* have happened!"

"It's *awful* and *terrible* that it happened!"

"My betrayer is a *totally rotten person* for betraying me!"

By disputing your dogmatic shoulding and musting about the betrayal, by seeing that it may have been quite wrong but it was not the worst thing in the world, and by accepting your betrayer as a sinner but still not agreeing with his or her sin, you achieve what REBT calls *unconditional other-acceptance* (UOA). You then can still consider the *betrayal* immoral (if that is your standard about it) even as you forgive the *person* who betrayed you. You thereby retain your concept of immorality — but *not* make yourself enraged and vindictive toward your betrayer. You will then stop your unforgiving obsessing and your own horrorizing about what happened and undisturbedly and productively *get on with your own life.*

◆ ◆ ◆

May 2001

Q *I read your writings on guilt and why we shouldn't ever feel that way. I tend to agree almost completely with your thoughts. But I had a question regarding guilt. Supposing that negative feelings in fact do come about due to*

*irrational thoughts; what about in cases where negative
feelings arise from rational thoughts? For example: If a
couple was having dinner and an argument ensued, later
one of the persons might feel bad, or guilty for putting the
other through that embarrassing situation. Another: If a
person in a committed relationship cheats on the other,
wouldn't feelings of guilt be warranted, and not from
irrational thoughts?*

◆

Rational Emotive Behavior Therapy (REBT) accepts
feelings of guilt — which we may call rational guilt — as
long as it involves your taking responsibility for your acts
that harm other people, but *not* putting *yourself* down *as a
person* for committing them. Rational or healthy guilt
consists of telling yourself, "I acted destructively and will
do my best to prevent myself from doing so again." With
this kind of guilt, you feel sorry and regretful for doing
harmful deeds.

Irrational or unhealthy guilt consists of telling yourself,
"I acted destructively and am therefore a *rotten* person!"
With this kind of guilt, you feel sorry for your *action* but
also self-downing, worthless, and depressed.

So you'd better take responsibility for, and deeply
regret, your wrong and harmful acts but not consider your
personhood as bad for performing them. Most people often
damn *themselves* as well as their *behaviors* for their wrong
doings, and REBT shows them how to rate their *actions* (or
thoughts and feelings) but not their *selves* as "bad."

◆ ◆ ◆

July 2000

Q *What is the role of feeling "shame" in human psychological disturbance as seen by REBT?*

◆

A Rational Emotive Behavior Therapy (REBT) views shame as consisting of two thoughts and feelings. First, a person has the *perception and thought* that he or she has committed a stupid, foolish, or immoral act — such as being rude to someone, dressing outlandishly, or stealing. Then he or she has rational, self-helping *beliefs* such as "I don't like what I did. I wish I had acted better, and I am sorry or displeased with my behavior and I had better correct it in the future." The rational or preferential belief will usually lead the wrong-doer to feel the healthy negative feeling of disappointment or regret about what he or she wrongly did — or feel shame about the wrong-doing but not shame or guilt about his or her total self for doing this act which is perceived as "bad" or "improper."

At the same time, however, a person may, first, view his or her action as a "wrong" or "immoral" act and also view his or her self as "bad" or "foolish." This person tends to think, "My action was wrong or improper and I am a bad or evil person because of my wrong action." Then this person denigrates her or his total self for this "wrong" behavior and feels immensely ashamed of her or his personhood. Using REBT, we try to show people that even when their behavior is, by all normal standards, "wrong," "stupid," or "immoral," they never have to feel intense shame by deprecating their entire personhood. They can merely make themselves feel quite sorry and disappointed about their actions (or inactions) without castigating themselves mercilessly, as usually happens when they bring on feelings of intense shame.

◆ ◆ ◆

September 1998

How can I rationally deal with the extreme anger and hurt that I am experiencing as a result of my significant other's affair, and the lies that went along with it? My attempts to think rationally are thwarted quickly by thoughts that lead to these sometimes (or often), extreme emotions. (I often feel rage.) I was also wondering if you have written about the issue of affairs and how to think and deal with them rationally? I have been in a lot of pain, but rationally speaking, I am sure a lot of it is avoidable. But how?? I would appreciate your insight.

◆

Hurt is largely the result of your noting your significant other's affair and telling yourself how wrong it is and how bad are the lies that went with it. These are your views and you are entitled to them. But you are also demanding that he *absolutely must not* be wrong and *absolutely should not* lie to you. You therefore create great hurt (self-pity) and rage. If you unconditionally accept him as a fallible human who easily does wrong things, you will still feel healthily sorry and disappointed in his *behavior,* but not condemn him totally *as a person,* for behaving this way. Good books on this subject are my books, *How to Control Your Anger Before It Controls You* and *A Guide to Rational Living*, Paul Hauck's *The Three Faces of Love*, Bill Borcherdt's *Head Over Heart in Love*, and Michael Broder's *Can Your Relationship Be Saved?*

◆ ◆ ◆

May 1999

Q *Until now I've believed that rage comes from demands, so I believed always it was irrational. But in your book,* Better, Deeper and — More Enduring Brief Therapy — *for which I congratulate you — I feel confused where you talk about a "right rage." Which rational discernments can we use for feeling with more precision the emotion of rage? Personally, when I feel rage, I change my demands for preferences and it disappears and becomes frustration.*

◆

A On page 69 of *Better, Deeper and More Enduring Brief Therapy*, I say, "Anger and rage are not always foolish. Particularly when people and institutions *do* treat you abominably, your revving up your fury may motivate, push, energize, and almost compel you to deal with stupidity and injustice."

Yes, but I also could have said that feeling strong annoyance and displeasure against other people's unfair acts would motivate you to deal with their *stupidity* and *injustice,* instead of totally damning *them* as people for being unfair. Rage rips up your gut and often pushes you to act stupidly and unfairly yourself. It creates feuds and wars instead of helping you deal adequately with the unfair behavior of others.

REBT is not opposed to strong feelings but to unhealthy feelings like panic, depression, and rage. Healthy negative feelings, as I point out in *Better, Deeper and More Enduring Brief Therapy,* can be motivating and action-oriented when you are treated badly. These can include *strong* feelings of displeasure, disappointment, and annoyance. As you rightly note, when you change your *demands* that others treat you well to *preferences* that they do so, your unhealthy rage disappears and is replaced by the healthy negative feeling of strong frustration.

◆   ◆   ◆

January 1998

Q *I am almost all the time worried about my looks and what would others think of me. I am sick of that and I don't want it anymore, but I can't help myself. What should I do?*

◆

A You can help yourself if you clearly see the Irrational Beliefs that are driving you to worry almost all the time about your looks and if you change them into Rational Beliefs. According to REBT theory, you are most probably taking your strong desires for good looks and for other people's approval and making them into absolute musts or needs. Thus, you are powerfully convincing yourself, "I *absolutely must* have very good looks and I *completely need* the approval of others." These Irrational Beliefs will almost certainly make you anxious, unless you actually have a *guarantee* that you always will look very well and will continually be approved by others. But such guarantees don't exist! You can convince yourself of the far more Rational Belief, "I *would prefer* to be attractive and be approved by others, but if I am not I can still accept myself and be a happy human," and you will most probably be less anxious. But you really *had* better solidly hold these Rational Beliefs, or similar ones, and not merely think that it would be lovely if you did hold them. *Wishing* you would have self-helping or Rational Beliefs will not make you hold them. That requires, as we show in REBT, a hell of a lot of work and practice!

◆ ◆ ◆

February 2000

Q My boyfriend suffers from social anxiety disorder. He
has never been diagnosed, but we've both read about it,
and it is quite obvious to us. The problem with him is
probably not as extreme as some of the cases I've read
about, but it is definitely disruptive and worrisome.
Despite being aware of his problem, and the effect the
problem has on both our lives, he refuses to go to therapy
or take any medications. My questions is, could the books
and/or audiotapes available on the market be of any help to
him (or me)?

◆

A Yes, there are many good books and audiotapes that
could help your boyfriend with his social anxiety. If you
and your boyfriend use these materials and really work at
the suggestions they include, he can considerably help
himself. Some of my own books include *A Guide to
Rational Living*, *How to Control Your Anxiety Before it
Controls You*, and *How to Make Yourself Happy and
Remarkably Less Disturbable.* My tapes include
Unconditionally Accepting Yourself and Others. Other
books and tapes which your boyfriend may find helpful
include, *Three Minute Therapy* by Michael Edelstein,
Overcoming Your Anxiety in the Shortest Period of Time by
Michael Broder, and *Your Perfect Right* by Robert Alberti
and Michael Emmons.

◆ ◆ ◆

February 2003

Q *Do you have any advice or reference materials that could be used in overcoming waking up in the middle of the night with anxiety? Here, one cannot do irrational confrontation (REBT) when the exact event cause(s) is unknown. Would deep muscle relaxation, self-hypnosis, etc., be an effective treatment for such anxiety and sleep disturbance?*

◆

A Whatever is the cause of your anxiety and the sleep disturbance that goes with it, deep muscle relaxation, self-hypnosis, and other kinds of relaxation have helped many people to distract themselves from their anxiety-provoking thoughts and therefore to go to sleep or go back to sleep. But the secret is that distraction methods do not cure anxiety problems, but often put them away — that is, put them to sleep — *temporarily.* That's enough! Their anxieties come back later — preferably during waking hours. But when you want to sleep, you can always use them effectively again.

Rational Emotive Behavior Therapy (REBT) has shown for many years that you usually make yourself anxious when you repetitively think in terms of absolute shoulds, oughts, and musts. Such as: "I *absolutely must* perform well or I am an *inadequate person!*" and "I *absolutely should* prevent unfortunate events from happening or else utter disaster would occur and that would be *terrible!*" You can largely cure anxiety, as REBT shows by turning your musts into preferences: "I'd *like very much* to perform well but I don't *have to!* I am never an *inadequate person* if I don't!" "I will try hard to ward off unfortunate events, but it is not *awful* if I don't, and I can still often be happy,

though not *as* happy as if I can't prevent them. Too bad!"
Do this strongly and you will make yourself less and less
anxious. Read our REBT books and listen to our tapes to see
how to do this!

If you use relaxing techniques, you can force yourself to
steadily think, feel, and do non-worrying things. You can say
"Om, om, om" over and over. You can make yourself relax
and relax your muscles. You can think of humorous things
or sing to yourself some of the rational humorous songs of
REBT. You can play tennis, golf, music, or have sex. Anything
that is really distracting? Yes, almost anything. Yoga,
meditation, watching your own thoughts, or contemplating
the universe. Focusing on the meaning of life. Again, almost
anything. But your concentration and your activity had
better be steady, strong, really focused, persistent. Otherwise,
you may easily go back to your worries.

I once had severe sleeping problems — including my
worrying about my not sleeping, which kept me fully
awake! Now, using REBT on myself, I practically never
worry! If the world comes to an end and I can't do anything
to stop it, too damned bad! Tough but not awful!

But I still at times keep myself awake with interesting,
enjoyable, creative thoughts. For a while I indulge in them.
But when I lie awake too long, I stop my interesting
thoughts. How? By forcing myself to say, no matter how
boring it is, "Relax, relax, relax, relax!" Persistently! If I
wander off, I force myself to return to, "Relax, relax, relax,
relax!" Strongly! If I think of something fascinating, I impel
myself back to, "Relax, relax, relax, relax!" Actively! I make
myself think *only* "Relax, relax, relax, relax!" Very simple.
But it soon drives out conflicting thoughts. Before I know
it, I sleep, sleep, sleep, sleep, sleep.

◆ ◆ ◆

September 1999

Q *Can REBT help with eating disorders? Have you had any success in this area?*

♦

A Yes, we see many clients at the Albert Ellis Institute in New York who have eating disorders and often help them considerably. We also give public and professional workshops showing how REBT helps people with such disorders. I have a book on that subject, *The Art and Science of Rational Eating*, which shows how REBT and Cognitive Behavior Therapy can be used with people who have eating disorders.

♦ ♦ ♦

June 2001

Q *I have recently read in the book* Learned Optimism, *by Martin Seligman, Ph.D., that depressives are more attuned to the realities of life's limitations and one's own limitations and shortcomings. As a depressive, I have always believed this to be true. My problem is that the book's premise is that to treat depression, one has to change the internal dialogue to one of optimism. I can't seem to reconcile the notion of "fooling myself" with optimism as a way of overcoming negative or limiting internal dialogue that may be based on the harshness of reality. What are your thoughts?*

♦

A I think that you are correct about using optimism to overcome feelings of depression. Pessimism, even when based on the realistic observation of your life's limitations and shortcomings, often goes too far — especially when people have a strong tendency, for biological and social learning reasons, to easily depress themselves. You pessimistically tell yourself, "My life has a number of unfortunate events and I am sure that they will keep happening and that I will not be able to deal with them. It's hopeless!" As Martin Seligman accurately points out, this pessimistic outlook can produce or exacerbate your depression.

Optimism is usually much better, because if you think that, despite actual and potential calamities, you can see misfortunes in a better light and see that you can handle them, you create an attitude that helps you deal better with adversities and you have the ability to ward them off in the future.

Optimism, however, can easily be taken to pollyannaish extremes. Thus, you can tell yourself, "Everything will happen for the best!" Or: "Day by day in every way, I'm getting better and better!" Or: "I am able to do anything I want to do!" This kind of unrealistic optimism, as you indicate, amounts to "fooling yourself" — because, as I point out in my books on Rational Emotive Behavior Therapy, you are a quite fallible human, and life will continue to bring you many misfortunes. As the Buddhists said 2500 years ago, "Life is a goddamn hassle!" REBT fully agrees.

Instead of pollyannaism, however you can choose to have several more realistic forms of optimism, such as these:

1. "I can't act infallibly and I can't control external conditions, but I can control my *reactions* to my mistakes and to unfavorable situations. I largely control my *emotional destiny*. I can *refuse* to take bad

conditions *too* seriously and can also refuse to *choose* to blame and damn myself for my depression."

2. "Yes, I have a good many shortcomings and my life has a number of limitations, but I can handle these adversities, often improve them, and expect good as well as bad things in the world. This, too shall pass!"

3. "Some exceptional misfortunes can happen to me — such as rape, cancer, hurricanes, or a war — but they will only occur rarely. If they do, I can still live and be reasonably happy. I can practically always find some activities that I really enjoy and keep looking for more of them — yes, even if unusual difficulties occur in my life!"

Optimism like this can be realistic rather than pollyannaish. I promote this down-to-earth kind of optimism in several of my books, which show how to use Rational Emotive Behavior Therapy for self-help. These include *A Guide to Rational Living* and *How to Make Yourself Happy and Remarkably Less Disturbable.*

So, don't give up on optimism — only on that which is taken to unrealistic extremes!

◆ ◆ ◆

July 1996

Q *Are so-called spiritual approaches to treating addictions really a form of REBT by encouraging a new way of thinking about the self and life?*

◆

A Yes, I think you are correct.

But "spiritual" has several meanings, some of which tend to contradict each other. Thus it first often means guided by the spirit or the soul, as distinguished from the body; spiritualistic or supernatural; devoted to religion or the church; sacred or ecclesiastical. But it also somewhat contradictorily means concerned with the intellect, or what is often thought of as the "better" or "high" part of the mind; showing much refinement of thought and feeling.

Rational emotive behavior therapy (REBT) follows this second kind of spirituality and tries to help people acquire a new way of thinking about themselves and about life. It encourages people to achieve unconditional self-acceptance (USA), unconditional acceptance of others (UOA), and high frustration tolerance (HFT). Along with Reinhold Niebuhr, it promotes the courage to change what people can change and to accept — though not to like — what they cannot change. It helps people work on a high degree of meaning and purposefulness.

REBT treats addictions, as well as the emotional disturbances of non-addicts, by showing people how to think, feel, and behave in a healthy, non-destructive manner. In these ways, REBT helps people to make themselves less disturbed and less disturbable, to be happier and more self-fulfilling, and to have a high degree of social interest.

◆ ◆ ◆

January 1999

I was wondering why you included the belief in life after death in the category of irrational beliefs. Millions of people hold onto this belief as the hope that there is something bigger than ourselves in this world. What is the ultimate purpose in living if there is no belief in God or life after death?

◆

A The belief in life after death is not necessarily irrational, as long as it is held undogmatically. Thus, you can say, "I believe there is life after death, but if there isn't any, that is unfortunate and I can still have purpose and meaning in this life." If you think that there *has* to be life after death to give meaning and purpose to this life, you are being dogmatic and risk disillusionment by later coming to believe, "But perhaps there is no life after death." You would then lose the meaning you have arbitrarily assumed *has* to exist. You'd better make your life meaning independent of the question of life after death.

◆ ◆ ◆

March 2000

Q *For many years already I have experienced depression. I have been treated for it, but my depression seems to originate from trying too hard to be a successful professional. It may seem a little simple, but I am an immigrant who left my country in search of a better life. What I always wanted was to be able to live comfortably and be able to give my family a piece of what they gave me. This whole idea has become an obsession and the feeling of worthlessness is getting worse with time. My question is, what kind of psychological problem do I have? Since Prozac was able to make me think a little clearer about my situation, would anything else help me think more rationally rather than any other alternative drug?*

◆

A You are probably correct in thinking that your depression at least partly originates from trying *too hard* to be a successful professional. You can by all means keep your goal of *wanting* to live comfortably and be able to give your family a piece of what they gave you. But you have raised this *healthy wanting* to a *dire needing*, and are obsessed with the idea that you *absolutely must* succeed and that you are *totally worthless* if you don't. This idea, like any *absolute must*, will tend to depress you — and then interfere with your succeeding. You can think more rationally in this respect by getting some Rational Emotive Behavior Therapy (REBT) and by reading some of my books, such as *A Guide To Rational Living* and *How To Make Yourself Happy and Remarkably Less Disturbable*.

◆ ◆ ◆

March 2002

Q *I was wondering if medication or therapy is better in treating depression. I know a lot of people who have been diagnosed with depression, but it seems like the drugs are just a quick fix for their problems, and that they could do something to change the fact that they are depressed. Can they?*

◆

A No one has found an exact and entirely reliable answer to your question about the value of medication and/or psychotherapy in treating depression. It is likely that there is no "true" or "correct" answer to this question, because there are several different kinds of depression, and afflicted people react uniquely to medication and to therapy.

First of all, let me discuss psychotherapy methods — there are many kinds available. Some of them are dangerous for many clients. Thus, classical psychoanalytic techniques help clients to obsess about their past history and to endlessly complain about the grim conditions of their present lives, and may therefore intensify their depressed feelings. Exceptionally expressive therapies — such as Gestalt, Reichian, and primal therapy — may also encourage clients to become more depressed, enraged and self-pitying, as a number of psychological studies have shown. Passive therapies — including classical psychoanalysis and person-centered therapies — may help some clients temporarily *feel* better, largely because they are pampered by their therapist, but rarely seem to help them *get* better by profoundly changing their negative philosophies, feelings, and actions.

Studies have shown that Rational Emotive Behavior Therapy (REBT) and Cognitive Behavior Therapy (CBT) are more effective than other therapies when used with severely depressed people — but also show that clients differ greatly in how they accept these therapies and how hard and persistently they work at applying their principles and practices. Some clients quickly take to them, steadily do their cognitive, emotional, and behavioral homework, and appreciably improve their depressed states, sometimes almost miraculously. Thus, by usage of the REBT techniques of unconditional self-acceptance (USA), unconditional other-acceptance (UOA), and unconditional life-acceptance (ULA) they make and they maintain remarkable mood gains. *Some* clients!!

Unfortunately not *all!* A good number of depressives are biologically afflicted — have what is called a chemical imbalance — and either benefit little from REBT and CBT or else take a considerable time to improve. Some clients improve only intermittently or never make much progress. Why? For a variety of reasons, which would take too long to discuss here.

Anyway, good psychotherapy has a generally good but still spotty record with severely depressed people. The same, alas, can be said for antidepressant medication. Prozac and other antidepressants and psychotropic medications may help some depressed people reasonably well, occasionally, temporarily, and inconsistently — or not at all! In fact, some of my clients insist, with some degree of accuracy, that various antidepressants do them much more harm than good. One depressed woman, for example, was being helped with Prozac but became so angry — probably because of the Prozac she was taking — that she often raged at her boyfriend and close relatives for minor infractions.

No, medication is not a complete answer for people's psychological problems, and many psychiatrists and other professionals counsel against it. Some of them, I am afraid, have a highly exaggerated and almost paranoid fear of medication; and some of the dissenters are fanatic naturists who even rant and rave against aspirin. On the other hand, some psychopharmacologists over-prescribe medication for practically all psychological problems, and are not to be trusted in that respect. Both negative and positive overgeneralizing is often rampant in regard to using medication for depression and other psychological troubles. No, drugs are not a quick fix for emotional disturbance — but all too frequently they can be overused.

What, then, to do if you or someone close to you suffers from heavy depression? Here are some guidelines to help depressed people:

1. See a psychiatrist or other licensed mental health professional who can properly diagnose depression.
2. Start to receive REBT, CBT, or some other form of psychotherapy that has regularly helped depressed people.
3. Work hard at the psychotherapy for a few months to see if there are benefits.
4. If little benefit comes from psychotherapy, try another psychotherapist.
5. See a good psychopharmacologist, who will advise some kind of medication(s), such as an antidepressant. Take this medication in conjunction with psychotherapy for a while, to see what works without serious side effects.
6. If one medication doesn't work or creates severe disadvantages, have it changed for a more suitable medication. If necessary, try several different medications to see which actually gives good results.
7. Finally, if no medication helps, keep working very hard with a compatible therapist to achieve unconditional self-acceptance (USA), unconditional other-acceptance (UOA), and unconditional life-acceptance (ULA), together with any other cognitive, emotive, and behavioral techniques that the therapist recommends.

Will all these steps assure you or your close friends of rarely being severely depressed? No, but they will in most cases appreciably help. If nothing works, they can at least help depressives to accept themselves and their life with their depressed moods. That in itself will be considerably beneficial.

August 2001

Q Isn't it rational and realistic to feel depressed about getting older? When I was young, much of my happiness came from looking forward to a (seemingly) endless future. But when you are older — what future? Diminishing capacity; finally, death. What are your thoughts on this? I'm sure they would be of interest to the aging baby-boomer population (of which I am a part).

◆

A No, it is rational and realistic if one chooses to feel the healthy negative feelings of regret, sorrow, and frustration when you see that you are getting older; but it is irrational — that is, self-defeating — to choose to make yourself depressed about growing old. You say that when you were young much of your happiness came from "looking forward to a (seemingly) endless future." But you were then, of course, unrealistic and utopian. All living creatures, including humans, get older and die. None, so far as I know, live forever. So you deluded yourself about having an endless — and presumably blissful — future. How more unrealistic than that could you have been?

Now that you are older, you see that you still have a future — maybe for thirty or forty years — but that it will probably be with diminishing capacity and definitely will include death. So you definitely *wish* that your future be as good as your earlier life may have been, and you *desire* that it be better and happier than it may actually become. Fine! If you only strongly wished that your older age be happy, you would then, again, feel sorry, regretful, and frustrated about the possibility of its being *less* satisfying than your younger life. But you would not be *depressed* about your older age unless you irrationally *insisted* that it *absolutely must not* be frustrating, that it *absolutely must* be as good as your earlier days, and that it *absolutely must not* end in death. Your choosing to make these unrealistic and self-defeating *demands* will result, most likely, in your depressing yourself about your older age — instead of your merely feeling healthily sad and sorry about some of its aspects. Depression, as my Rational Emotive Behavior Therapy teachings and writings have pointed out since 1955, doesn't stem from your strongly *wanting* maximum enjoyment and minimal pain in the one life you'll ever have, but from your irrationally *insisting* that you absolutely *must* get what you want and also *must not* get what you dislike.

So, let us admit that older age has some real disadvantages. But, as I point out in my book with Emmett Velten, *Optimal Aging: Getting Over Getting Older,* it also has its assets and advantages. Moreover, if you genuinely dislike aging but still use Rational Emotive Behavior Therapy to stubbornly refuse to depress yourself about it, you can most probably delight in a good many years to come. Try constructive healthy thoughts, feelings, and behaviors about growing older and you may actually enjoy many aspects of it!

◆　◆　◆

July 2001

Q Is there a rational way to accept death? My grandmother died a week ago. I am having a hard time creating rational thoughts in response to her death. It seems cruel and unjust that people should die. Can you help?

◆

A There are several rational — meaning, self-helping — ways to accept death, including the following ones:

1. Clearly distinguish between *disliking* or feeling *displeased* with some "bad" event and making yourself *nonaccepting* or *horrified* about it. It is normal to heartily *dislike* or *hate* hurricanes, injustices, bigotry, cruelty, murders, wars, and the deaths of people you care for. You would be acting in a pretty crazy way if you *preferred* or *liked* them. Anything that you see as sabotaging your goals, values, or interest, or anything you think works against your community or social interest, you view with sorrow or regret. You strongly *wish* that it didn't occur. Why not? Rational Emotive Behavior Therapy (REBT), therefore, assesses practically all your dislikes or displeasures as *healthy* or *helpful* negative feelings. They will usually aid you to get more of what you want and less of what you abhor in life. Good!

2. When you raise your aversion to death (or almost any other abhorrence) to an *insistence* that, because it is undesirable, it *absolutely must not* exist and that it is *terrible* that it does exist, you self-defeatingly *demand* that what you *want* must be and that what you *detest* must not be. But by raising your *displeasure* and *sorrow* at death (or any other misfortune) to a *command* that it cease to be, you may refuse to accept grim realities, make yourself unhealthily enraged or depressed (instead of healthily sad) because of their existence, and make yourself inclined to suffer *more* than you would suffer if you merely disliked them. By nonacceptance, you *increase* rather than *minimize* your suffering about unfortunate things that you cannot change.

3. As Reinhold Niebuhr wisely said, you had better change unfortunate things that you can change, accept (but not like) those that you cannot change, and have the wisdom to know the difference between the two. Death, once it has occurred, is of course unchangeable. However much you "horrorize" yourself about it, you *still* cannot change it. Not a bit! So where does your horribilizing and terribilizing get you?

4. You may choose to *view* the death of your grandmother (or anyone else) as "cruel" and "unjust" but that seems in some way unreasonable. For wouldn't it be quite "cruel" to keep people like your grandmother living until they were, say, two hundred years old and unable to do practically anything they really enjoy because of the normal disabilities and deficiencies of extreme old age?

5. Moreover, if people "uncruelly" and "justly" lived forever, our planet would obviously soon be incredibly overpopulated. How "fair" would that be to the surviving people — and to the millions who would have to remain unborn to provide room for their survival? No animal or plant species, including humans, lives forever; and that is why *new* recruits to every species are able to be born. Give that matter some deep thought!

6. Even if it is truly unfair and cruel that fine people like your grandmother inevitably die without "deserving" to do so, who says that the world *has* to be fair and nice? What we call "Nature" is frequently harmful. Whether we like it or not, we had therefore better accept that fact, as gracefully as we can, and uncomfortably — but not horrifyingly — try to change it or put up with it. What else can we sensibly do?

7. If the death of your grandmother (and of any other loved person) reminds you that you will someday die yourself, and you are terrified of that happening, you are then probably telling yourself that it is *awful* to no longer continue your life, that perhaps you will suffer in some kind of afterlife — and that that would be *terrible*. Instead, however, you can convince yourself that it is *damned inconvenient* for you to end this life but, in all probability you will not even *know* how inconvenient it is when you are *dead* — because you will most probably be totally unfeeling. Your "afterlife" will almost certainly be exactly the same as your state of being before your parents conceived you — that is, your sensations and feelings will be zero. Yes, zero.

8. You had better convince yourself that if you do have an afterlife, it will most probably be no better or worse than your present life. There is no evidence that it will be "bad" or "miserable" — and even if it is, worrying about it *now* will only help ruin your *present* aliveness. Making yourself anxious about your possibly "horrible" afterlife will hardly make it better! You can only be sure that your *present* life exists and is potentially enjoyable. Concentrate on making it so!

These, it seems to me, are some rational, sensible, and healthy thoughts and feelings you can have about the "cruel" and "inhuman" problems of death. I am sure that there are still other rational conclusions you can make about the sad fact that you and your loved ones will finally die. Try out some of the thoughts that I have suggested — and some of those you can construct for yourself.

◆ ◆ ◆

December 1996

Q *Co-dependency was the "buzz word" of the 1990s, but isn't it just people caring for people who are in trouble? Is there really a condition known as "co-dependency"? How does REBT make a difference in this so-called condition?*

◆

A Co-dependency definitely exists but often has been used too loosely in the literature. When properly defined it means that a person is first dependent on others' love and approval and considers himself or herself inadequate or worthless if missing such approval. Vast numbers of people have this serious problem. A co-dependent, however, is so abysmally dependent that he or she chooses as a partner another very needy person — such as an alcoholic who needs to be taken care of — and remains attached to this person in spite of getting little love or care in return. Both partners are then quite dependent on each other. While dependency is very common, co-dependency is much less common, but is fairly frequent among serious addicts and their partners. REBT shows both dependents and co-dependents that love and approval are important aspects of human relationships, but are not absolutely necessary for one to feel worthy and adequate.

◆ ◆ ◆

December 1999

Q *REBT promotes unconditional self-acceptance (USA) and unconditional other-acceptance (UOA). Since human beings are imperfect creatures, how is it possible to achieve this, or do we just strive for "perfection" and never quite hit the mark?*

◆

A First of all, let us not insist upon *perfect* unconditional self-acceptance (USA), *perfect* unconditional other-acceptance (UOA), or *perfect* anything else. Second, as you point out, we can *strive for* "perfection" without *having* to reach it. Trying for it is interesting and fascinating. *Needing* to achieve it is deadly!

◆ ◆ ◆

November 2001

Q *I have recently read a book by the Dalai Lama. He affirms that he loves unconditionally all his fellow human beings as he shares with them common features that are more important than all the differences. These common features are the fact that we all have the same physical structure and a mind using the same working principles; the fact that we were all born in the same way and similarly we'll die; that we all share the same life goal that is to achieve happiness. If we keep in mind the common things we share, all the differences (i.e., religion, sex, opinions, etc.) become minor issues.*

I think that there are important similarities between the Dalai Lama's philosophy, the Christian philosophy of loving the other, and the REBT philosophy of Unconditional Other-Acceptance (UOA).

My question is as follows. Although in principle I truly believe that the unconditional acceptance of others (UOA) philosophy is rational from the empirical, logical and pragmatic point of view, I find it sometimes difficult to live it in practice (especially after the tragic events of September 11, 2001). I think that my beliefs need to be reinforced from the emotional and behavioral point of view, but I cannot find ways to do so. Can you suggest to me ways to absorb and live UOA in day-to-day life?

◆

A Yes, as you and many other readers have noticed, there are important similarities between the Dalai Lama's philosophy, the Christian philosophy of loving the other, and the REBT philosophy of Unconditional Other-Acceptance (UOA). Many readers of my books, especially *A Guide to Rational Living*, and of the Dalai Lama's writings, especially *The Art of Happiness*, have remarked on the unusual similarities between our views. Also, many Bible readers have noted REBT's endorsement of the Christian philosophy, "accept the sinner but not the sin." David Lima, Inc., and the Albert Ellis Institute have submitted a proposal for a meeting between His Holiness the Dalai Lama and myself to discuss our philosophic similarities and it is hoped that this meeting will be arranged when the Dalai Lama next visits the United States.

Our proposal for a meeting where the Dalai Lama and I discuss our common views includes twenty attitudes and practices that we share about reducing emotional disturbance and achieving human happiness. Among these mutual philosophies, we list "unconditional acceptance of self and others leads to less fear, more openness and honesty, and more authentic relationships." This is a core REBT theory and practice.

Many people subscribe in theory to this REBT view but, like yourself, find it difficult to live it in practice (especially after the recent tragic terroristic events). I have attached an essay on the REBT approach to terrorism, which is posted on the Institute web site, at www.rebt.org. By all means read this essay.

Rational Emotive Behavior Therapy has always been rational but also includes many emotional-evocative and behavioral exercises that you can use to reinforce your rational thinking. For example, it shows you how to use my famous "shame-attacking exercise" and Maxie Maultsby Jr.'s "rational emotive imagery." These are both behavioral and emotional techniques that you can practice to absorb and live with unconditional other-acceptance (UOA), the view that the Dalai Lama also endorses. They are described in detail, along with other REBT emotional and behavioral methods, in several of my books and cassettes, such as, *Feeling Better, Getting Better, Staying Better* and *Overcoming Destructive Beliefs, Feelings, and Behaviors.* By all means try these REBT and other exercises and let me know how they work to implement your rational, peace-oriented philosophy! If my proposal to discuss our mutual outlook with the Dalai Lama is arranged, we shall of course announce it on our REBT website: www.rebt.org

◆ ◆ ◆

August 2000

Q *In what ways can REBT enhance the spiritual life of a person?*

◆

A REBT can enhance the spiritual life of people in several ways, including these:

1. Helping people to develop unconditional other-acceptance (UOA) for all humans, including those who make serious mistakes and/or are unkind and immoral to other people.

2. Helping people to achieve a vital absorbing interest on a long-term basis that gives unusual meaning in their lives.

3. Helping people to have unconditional self-acceptance (USA) but at the same time to devote themselves to humanitarian goals and purposes.

4. Helping people to accept the challenge of being less disturbable and intent on an enjoyable life even when they are sorely afflicted with unfortunate circumstances.

5. Helping people to have unusual integrity and honesty with themselves and others, in spite of the criticism from others and themselves that they may receive.

6. Helping people be realistically optimistic and have considerable hope for the future.

◆ ◆ ◆

December 2001

Since the incident of September 11, 2001, Muslims are *unfortunately labeled by some as people who support terrorism and injustice. I'm a Muslim and I strongly disagree with this notion. I feel that most of us have been clouded with anger and irrational thinking, which has led others to believe that Muslim teaching encourages terrorist action. The Koran is actually against such actions, and even condemns them.*

I notice that the principles of REBT are actually not in contrast with many aspects of the Koran. Yet many people who believe that they are rational do not believe the essence of the Koran. They continue to label Muslims as a non-rational community. What is your comment?

◆

A Yes, Muslims are unfortunately labeled by some individuals as people who support terrorism and injustice — especially since the incident of September 11. This kind of over-generalizing about a large group of people because of the behavior of a few was strongly opposed by Alfred Korzybski in his 1933 book, *Science and Sanity*. It has also been opposed by Rational Emotive Behavior Therapy (REBT) since I originated it in January 1955. REBT, like the Christian philosophy of accepting the sinner but not the sin, holds that terroristic activity is immoral, but refuses to completely condemn all terrorists, all Muslims, or all humans who commit inhumane acts. It strongly teaches unconditional other acceptance (UOA) along with unconditional self-acceptance (USA). This means that we encourage all individuals to accept *all* people, *whether or not* they act well, and also to accept themselves, their personhood, *whether or not* they perform competently.

According to social and cultural custom, many human acts are individually and socially good or helpful; and many human acts are bad or unhelpful. Terroristic actions are considered by most of us to be wrong or immoral — as stated in the Koran and in the Jewish and Christian Bibles. But, as Korzybski and REBT both say, people *are not* their acts, even when they irresponsibly commit them. They sometimes *do* unethical or socially evil *things*; but they *are not* evil or damnable *persons*. They do thousands of bad (and good) acts, but they cannot accurately be labeled as *bad or good people*.

As you note, many so-called rational people disbelieve the essence of Koran — as well as the essence of the Jewish and Christian Bibles — and keep labeling Muslims as non-rational communities. This is what the philosopher Wilford

Quine called a serious category error. It amounts to bigotry
— the same kind of bigotry that terrorists exhibit.

◆　◆　◆

September 2001

*How would one go about using REBT in order to cope
and to help others cope with the tragic events that took
place on September 11, 2001? I am looking for a proactive
way to deal with the brutality of this act, but find that my
irrational beliefs and "shoulds" are getting in my way.*

◆

Your irrational beliefs and shoulds that get in your way
probably include:

1. "I absolutely *must* be able to figure out a way to stop
   terrorists from acting so brutally and killing and
   maiming so many people, and there is something
   very weak and inadequate about me because I can't
   find a way to stop this kind of terrorism."
2. "The terrorists and their backers have perpetrated
   some of the worst deeds imaginable; this makes them
   completely rotten people who *should absolutely be
   exterminated* — quickly — since only killing all of
   them will stop this deed from happening again."
3. "Because the world is so full of cruel violence and
   terrorism, it is a totally despicable place and I cannot
   continue to live in it and be at all happy."

These ideas are irrational because, as Alfred Korzybski
noted, they are unrealistic and illogical overgeneralizations
that render people "unsane." My 1962 book, *Reason and
Emotion in Psychotherapy*, showed that all three of these
beliefs — and many similar absolutistic shoulds and musts

— lead you (and innumerable other people) to make yourself not only very sad and displeased with the terrorists' abominable behavior, but also to dysfunctionally overwhelm yourself with panic, rage, and depression. Thus, the first of these irrational beliefs will cause you to loathe your entire self, or personhood, not to only deplore your weakness and inadequacy to halt terrorism. The second of these irrational beliefs will make you thoroughly despise the terrorists (and all other people who do cruel deeds) and consume yourself with rage. The third of these irrational beliefs will make you hopelessly depressed about the present and future state of the world and encourage you to obsessively contemplate — and perhaps actually commit — suicide.

Ironically, these three self-defeating *shoulds* and *musts* are probably very similar to those held by the terrorists of September 11, 2001, who unsanely killed themselves and thousands of innocent people for what they considered a sacred holy crusade. They first considered themselves powerless because they could not stop America from "cruelly" siding with their enemies; and they therefore felt that they *absolutely had to* punish America to prove that they themselves were powerful and worthwhile individuals. Second, they devoutly believed that Americans *absolutely must not* oppose their position and that *all Americans are complete devils* who deserve to be wiped out. Third, they dogmatically convinced themselves there is no use living in and trying to lead a happy life in such a totally evil world; and therefore, by killing the infidels, they would attain eternal, blissful life. So, with these unsane beliefs, they enthusiastically killed themselves, along with countless innocent people.

If you and the rest of American and world citizens keep reinforcing your irrational beliefs, you will enrage yourself against the terrorists and their backers and in the process will likely encourage them to increase their fury against Americans and other people who oppose them, and will encourage more retaliation by them and by us again, until the cycle of retaliation precipitates a world-wide war and quite possibly the end of our planet. As ancient lore and modern history have amply shown, love begets love and hatred and violence beget increased hatred and violence — with no end in sight!

You ask how REBT would help you cope with and help others cope with the tragic events of September 11. That requires a long answer, which I can only briefly summarize here.

First, you can use REBT to teach yourself — and all others — *unconditional self-acceptance.* That is, you fully accept yourself with all of your warts and flaws, while heartily disliking and doing your best to change some of your self-defeating behaviors and poor behavior toward others.

Second, you can use REBT to *unconditionally accept all other people* as persons, no matter how badly they act. You can, of course, firmly try to induce them, in a variety of ways, to change their self-sabotaging and immoral thoughts, feelings, and actions. In Christian terms, you unconditionally accept all *sinners* but not their *sins.* Ultimately, some behaviors may require sanctions or imprisonment for individuals.

Third, you *unconditionally accept life,* with its immense problems and difficulties, and teach yourself to have high frustration tolerance. As Reinhold Niebuhr said, you strive to change the unfortunate things that you can change, to accept (but not to like) those that you cannot change, and to have the wisdom to know the difference.

If you achieve a good measure of these three REBT philosophies — that is, unconditional self-acceptance, unconditional other-acceptance, and unconditional life-acceptance — will you therefore be able to convince terrorists to change their absolutistic bigoted ways? Not exactly. But you will cope much better with terrorism, help others to cope with it, and model behavior that can, if you strongly encourage it to be followed around the world, eventually reduce it to a minimum. This will take many years to effect, and will require immense and persistent educational efforts by you and others to promote peaceful and cooperative solutions instead of hateful and destructive "solutions" to serious national and international difficulties. If we fail to work on our own belief systems to produce this long-term purpose, we will only insure renewed terrorism for decades, and perhaps centuries, to come.

Are you willing to keep relentlessly working for REBT's recommendations for self-peace, peace to other humans, and peace to the world? If so, you may help people of good will to think, plan, and construct eventual answers to terrorism and many other serious world problems.

◆ ◆ ◆ ◆

Ask Albert Ellis...
"About
Doing REBT"

Answers for Therapists.

REBT Compared to Other Therapies

May 1997

Q *Do you feel that REBT can be used as a sole orientation to psychotherapy? If not, to what extent is eclecticism helpful or harmful? A major trend in today's graduate programs is the emphasis put on developing an eclectic therapeutic style.*

◆

A "Eclectic" has several different definitions. REBT is in some respects very "eclectic" because it uses a large number of cognitive, emotive, and behavioral methods, some of which are unique to REBT but some of which — such as encounter, experimental, and existential methods — are adapted from other systems of psychotherapy. It also holds that clients have unique personalities and individual tendencies to react to therapy, therefore REBT — as I show in my books, *Better, Deeper, and More Enduring Brief Therapy, Rational Emotive Behavior Therapy: A Therapist's Guide,* and *Reason and Emotion in Psychotherapy* — urges its practitioners to use different therapeutic styles and techniques with different clients. However, like practically all therapies, REBT has its own unique theory, and its methods usually follow and implement that theory. Its theory has some common elements with other major therapy theories, but also has several significant differences. Eclecticism can be helpful or harmful, depending on how it is defined and used. REBT is probably more eclective and integrative than any of the major systems of therapy, except Arnold Lazarus' multimodal therapy, with which it significantly overlaps.

◆ ◆ ◆

March 1999

Your usage of the word "irrational" needs to be clarified for me, and perhaps others. In describing wrong-headed or self-defeating behavior or thought patterns, are you saying that such action or thought is irrational from the point of view of the client's well-being and personality? Are you using the term in an absolute sense, independently of the client's total situation? The truth of the statement, "That is irrational," rests within the context of the client's life goals and purposes. There is not much difference between irrational and self-defeating. Does this description agree with your own intent and usage? Please clarify.

◆

Yes, in Rational Emotive Behavior Therapy (REBT), as you point out, there is not much difference between *irrational* and *self-defeating* behaviors. Each of us has basic life goals and purposes — especially, to stay alive and relate enjoyably to ourselves, with other people, and in educational, vocational, and recreational pursuits. We want to get what we want when we want it, and to avoid getting what we don't want. We desire to gain satisfaction and to avoid pain, disease, and undue trouble and restriction. Therefore, we are *rational, functional,* or *self-helping* when we attempt to fulfill these goals, and we are *irrational, dysfunctional,* or *self-defeating* when we sabotage them.

REBT, as you note, doesn't use the term "rational" in any absolute sense but applies it to the individual's and the group's *chosen* desires and preferences. What is "good" or "rational" for one person or group may be "bad" or "irrational" for another.

However, since humans are social creatures and normally live in and importantly depend upon the acceptance and cooperation of other members of their social group, "rational" also means getting along effectively with and not seriously interfering with the survival or the goals of this group. It includes having consideration for and caring for the welfare of others — or what Alfred Adler called *social interest.* Total absorption in only your own goals and purposes to the exclusion of your group's interests would tend to be self-defeating — and so would be total devotion to group interests and desires and no consideration of your own. If you *choose* to live in a social community — rather than, say, to be a hermit — your very choice is an important purpose. Therefore, rational, self-helping living had better strike a two-sided balance between taking good care of yourself and taking care of others.

As John Donne said, "No (hu)man is an island." Rational or effective living includes being kind to your own basic goals and purposes — as well as to those of others. Both!

◆ ◆ ◆

January 2002

I am currently writing an essay on the main differences between cognitive and psychodynamic counseling. I'm having trouble realizing the purpose of cognitive. I would appreciate your help. What is the connection, or rather, what do you (REBT) owe to psychoanalysis? I fail to see the connection. In fact, you're the only one that can get me to even begin thinking that there is a connection.

◆

A In my book, *Overcoming Resistance: A Rational Emotive Behavior Therapy Integrating Approach*, I show how Rational Emotive Behavior Therapy can be integrated with psychodynamic theories. Briefly, Freud was a genius who realized that we have unconscious — as well as conscious — ideas and feelings and that we had better realize both forms of thinking and feeling so that we can change them for more effective forms. However, Freud wrongly thought that our unconscious thoughts and feelings are deeply repressed and difficult to understand. Actually, they are just below the surface of consciousness and REBT shows you how to find them and change them.

Psychoanalytic writing says that if you know your unconscious thoughts and feelings, your insight into them will get you to change them. Well, it won't! Instead, you first have to see your unconscious thoughts and feelings, particularly your absolutistic shoulds and musts. Then you have to use several REBT cognitive, emotional, and behavioral methods (which psychoanalysis mainly omits) to work very hard at changing your *shoulds*, *oughts*, and *musts* to realistic *preferences*. If you steadily work and practice at doing so, you will ultimately feel better, get better, and stay better, as I say in my book, *Feeling Better, Getting Better, Staying Better*. Psychoanalysis has some good teachings but, ironically enough, is superficial, unless it also includes the thinking, feeling, and behavioral methods of REBT and Cognitive Behavior Therapy (CBT). I demonstrate these methods in detail in another of my books, *Overcoming Destructive Beliefs, Feelings, and Behaviors.*

◆ ◆ ◆

January 1997

Most psychodynamic therapies assume the traditional unconsciousness processes, namely id, ego, and superego. However, no proof exists. I have problems accepting a whole system of theories based on nothing. How does REBT view the unconscious processes?

◆

REBT agrees with psychoanalysis that people often have thoughts, feelings, and even behaviors of which they are not fully aware but that nonetheless significantly affect their lives. Freud believed that many of their unconscious thoughts are deeply repressed and almost impossible to bring to consciousness. REBT holds that deeply repressed thoughts do exist — usually because people would severely blame themselves if they were aware of them. But most unconscious thoughts — particularly strong *musts* and *shoulds* that lead to anxiety and depression — are just below the level of consciousness and can fairly easily be figured out and understood by looking for them. They then can be questioned, disputed, and changed. REBT often deals with clients' unconscious thoughts and feelings but quite differently than psychodynamic therapies do. My book with Robert Harper, *A Guide to Rational Living*, gives examples of discovering and disputing unconscious irrational beliefs.

◆ ◆ ◆

November 2002

Q *I understand how Rational Emotive Behavior Therapy is used in individual and group therapy sessions but how is it used in family therapy sessions? Can it be used with other systems, such as Bowenian Therapy, Family Systems Therapy, and Structural Therapy?*

◆

A REBT is used during family therapy sessions by first showing all the family members that they usually assume that the other members upset and disturb them by behaving "wrongly" or "badly" but that this assumption is only partly true. One family member may indeed behave disruptively or unjustly, because this frequently happens in families — as almost anyone outside the family would attest. However, the REBT family practitioner points out to all the members present that it is not *just* one member acting "badly" that upsets another, but *also* what the upset person tells himself or herself *about* the "wrong" member's behaviors.

Take, for example, the problem of anger, which is the one most often raised in family therapy. Johnny, let us say, is not doing his homework and keeps hitting his younger sister, Mary, and both his parents (not to mention Mary) are very angry at him. I, as a family therapist, soon ascertain that Johnny is indeed rebelling against his parental standards, is failing in school, and is abusing his sister. But I quickly show the whole family, that although Johnny's behavior is *undesirable,* it alone cannot *make* them furious with him. Actually, *they create* their rage at his wrong behavior (A) by adding their strong demands (B) that "Johnny absolutely *must not* act that wrong way!" Their feelings of rage then erupt as a Consequence (C). They therefore have a *choice* of what REBT calls *healthy* negative feelings (e.g., sorrow and disappointment) instead of *unhealthy* feelings (e.g., anger and hatred) at Johnny and his behavior. Moreover, their objecting to Johnny's behavior seems sensible enough and may induce him to improve it. But their damning and making themselves enraged at *Johnny* will likely help him become equally angry, increase his rebellion, and hence encourage him to become more disruptive. So, I try to get the father, mother, and Mary to see, perhaps even during my first session with this family, that even if Johnny's behavior is quite wrong, he is not a *bad person* or a *louse* for committing it; and if they stop damning *him* and merely disapprove of his *acts*, they may possibly help him behave better.

In other words, I teach this family, from the first session onward, unconditional other-acceptance (UOA) instead of rage at and damnation of Johnny — and I may start to create much less anger in this family.

At the same time, I may try to show Johnny that his parents' strict rules about homework do not *make* him rebellious and angry, but that these rules *plus* his own shoulds and musts ("they must not treat me in that overdemanding way!") upset him, make him overly rebellious, and perhaps also abusive of his sister, (who may possibly conform more to parental rules and therefore be "unfairly" favored by the parents).

As I show all the family members that they invariably *choose* to upset themselves about the other members and their "misdeeds," I also teach them several REBT-oriented methods of communicating and cooperating with each other that are likely to get them better results and aid family harmony. These methods are described in detail in my books on relationship, such as *Making Intimate Connections* and *Dating, Mating, and Relating*.

Other systems of family therapy — such as Family Systems Therapy, Bowenian Therapy, and Structural Therapy — can be used with REBT, as long as the therapist includes the central REBT concept that family members do not *merely* upset each other but tell themselves unrealistic and rigid shoulds, oughts, and musts *about* other members' actions and thereby frequently *make themselves* angry, depressed, and anxious. If REBT cognitive, emotive, and behavioral techniques are used with family members to help them see and surrender their irrational beliefs, I think that almost all kinds of family therapy would be considerably improved. Let us hope so!

◆ ◆ ◆

June 1998

Q *What are some of the limitations and criticisms of REBT?*

◆

A The main criticism is that it is too rational and doesn't deal efficiently with emotions. This is incorrect, because REBT says that thinking, feeling, and behaving are not separate, but are interrelated and go with each other. Therefore, it includes many emotional and many behavioral methods, in addition to its realistic and logical disputing of people's irrational beliefs. It is probably the most experiential and emotive therapy of all the cognitive behavior therapies that are now popular.

◆ ◆ ◆

September 1996

Q *Much has been written recently about REBT being a distinct form of cognitive behavior therapy. However, I would like you to discuss the existential aspects of this theory. You once called yourself an existentialist, and as an Associate Fellow and practitioner of REBT, I consider myself to practice an existential therapy. Can a therapy be cognitive-behavioral and existentialist at the same time?*

◆

A Existentialism has many aspects and schools and is therefore hard to define precisely. Some of its main ideas which I hold and which I incorporate into my own practice of Rational Emotive Behavior Therapy (REBT) are these:

1. The universe and human life seem to have no absolute meaning or "truth with a capital T." We humans give it meaning and purpose.

2. We have our existence or Being in the world and constantly interact with and are related to other people and things. They importantly affect us and we significantly influence them.

3. Although we have distinct biological and social limitations, we also have a significant amount of choice. We can choose our goals, meanings, and purposes and choose to work — or not to work — at achieving them.

4. We can passively accept our existence or actively keep constructing and reconstructing it. We are natural constructivists and problem-solvers, but we also are easily self-defeating. When we choose to create profound meanings and long-range goals for ourselves and our community we tend to lead more satisfying and less disturbed lives. Faith in our

choices and commitment to implementing them is
usually helpful to our existence.

5. We had better care strongly for our own survival and
happiness and for that of the community in which we
choose to live. Not *either/or* but *both/and!*

6. We can choose to evaluate and accept ourselves
conditionally — because we do something well — or
unconditionally — just because we choose to do so
because we are human and alive. REBT holds that
unconditional self-acceptance (USA) and
unconditional other-acceptance (UOA) usually lead to
less emotional disturbance and more fulfillment than
do conditional acceptance of self and others.

◆ ◆ ◆

July 2002

*Would you agree with me in describing your approach
as applied* Radical Existentialism? *I find that what you
trigger in the client is the humane capacity to transcend
oneself, to exercise free will, as suggested by existentialists.
Radical, because you suggest not only to change behavior
and cognition but also emotions/feelings and intensity of
affect by the free will (though the change of emotions,
feelings and intensity of affect is/can be with cognition as
agent).*

◆

Yes, Rational Emotive Behavior Therapy (REBT) can be
described as "radical existentialism." It follows several
existential theories and procedures:

1. It is a psychotherapy that emphasizes human *choice*,
as existentialism does. People are not merely

conditioned or trained by their family and their culture to think, feel, and behave in certain ways. They also have a good degree of agency or "free will," which enables them to *choose* much of their behavior. They are limited by their biology and their upbringing, but they *also* have many possibilities they can select or not select. Hundreds of them, during their lifetime!

2. Even when they choose to behave in a certain way, people almost always have the ability to *re*-choose and to *change* their thoughts, feelings, and actions. Not completely — but considerably! REBT strongly shows them that they have these choices — providing that they consistently *work and practice* to make and remake them. It's *easy* for them to fall back on dysfunctional behaving. But they can recoup and recover — if they *think* they can!

3. Another way of stating this is to say that humans, by birth and social training, are *constructivists*. But they are prone to create destructive behaviors as well; and they can reconstruct their destructive doings. Again, with forceful deciding, determining, and *acting* to do so.

4. Most existential psychotherapies are philosophical and emotive, but REBT is pioneeringly and strongly cognitive, emotional, *and* behavioral. It especially shows people how to mindfully think, to think about their thinking, and to think about thinking about their thinking — which, of all animals, they are probably the only one that can forcefully do all three kinds of philosophizing. But, as you note in your question, it always combines emotional and behavioral methods with cognitive methods, so that it encourages people to think emotionally and actively,

to feel cognitively and actively, and to act thinkingly and emotionally. All three!

5. REBT is optimistic and encouraging — since, once again, people *can* change their choices and choose their changes. But REBT realistically emphasizes human individuals and social limitations and restrictions, and pushes people to *un*comfortably push their butts in order to comfortably and enjoyably change and stay changed.

As *radical existentialism*, REBT especially teaches and encourages people with active-directive, no-nonsense-about-it therapy to *choose* to change and fulfill themselves, out of a great number of possibilities they have for *experimental* living. Try it and see!

◆ ◆ ◆

October 2000

I have been in therapy for about three years now with an Existentialist therapist. He has helped me to some extent. However, I seem not to be satisfied. It seems to me I need more direct and challenging therapy — a therapy that will help me get more in touch with my feelings, rather than depend on everyday experiences in life and learn how I respond to those. I would prefer to be guided in therapy to deal more challengingly with how I feel about myself as a person and how to interact more effectively with others. Also, to create a more dynamic interaction with the therapist. Should I endeavor to discuss this with my present therapist and see if even REBT could be put into effect? Also, how can I find a REBT therapist near my home?

◆

Rational Emotive Behavior Therapy (REBT) is one of the
existential psychotherapies, but it is usually done in a
highly active-directive manner. It is direct and challenging
and also uses a number of emotional-evocative exercises
that deal with your feelings. Many existential therapists
mistakenly believe that people like you are innately
constructivists and can fairly easily change themselves as a
result of meaningful, philosophical discussions with a
therapist. Actually, damned few of them can do this! Most
clients, including those treated with existential therapy,
require a very active-directive, questioning and challenging
therapist, who works with them to use a number of
cognitive, emotive, and behavioral techniques, and who
closely monitors the homework assignments that they
agree to take. This is what is done in REBT.

Yes, by all means discuss this with your therapist and
see if he could combine his existential philosophy with
more directive and challenging REBT methods. If you want
a Rational Emotive Behavior Therapist or a Cognitive
Behavior Therapist near you, call the Albert Ellis Institute
in New York at (212) 535-0822 and ask if one is available. If
not, you can arrange to have phone sessions with me or
with one of our other REBT qualified practitioners by
calling this same number and arranging for such a session.

◆ ◆ ◆

November 2000

*As a student of Ayn Rand's philosophy of Objectivism,
I'm wondering if you're aware of just how closely REBT
matches this philosophy? Objectivism focuses on rational*

self-interest, setting rational goals and striving to achieve them, thinking rationally, using logic to solve everyday problems, achieving personal happiness (as opposed to living for the sake of serving/ pleasing/ impressing others), and the fact that our emotions stem from our thoughts. Were any elements of REBT specifically derived from Objectivism, or is the striking similarity just coincidence?

◆

Yes, REBT matches the semi-rational philosophy of Ayn Rand's Objectivism in many respects just as it overlaps with some of the rational philosophies of Aristotle, Kant, Dewey, Russell, and other philosophers. But I was not influenced by Ayn Rand, though I read *The Fountainhead* in the 1940s and found some good rationality in it. I also saw that she carried some of her ideas to super-romantic, unrealistic, and irrational extremes. I was friendly with her spokesman, psychologist Nathaniel Branden in 1957 (I had already created Rational Emotive Behavior Therapy [REBT] in 1955), and at first thought he was pretty rational, but I then realized that both he and Ayn Rand took practically all their sensible ideas to irrational, semifascistic, and — ironically enough — religious extremes. I voiced my views to Nathaniel and suggested that I debate publicly with Ayn Rand on "Rational Emotive Behavior Therapy vs. Objectivist Psychology." As I expected, she refused to debate with me but agreed to have Branden do so. We had our debate on May 26, 1967 before 1100 people, most of them followers of Objectivism. I was in good shape and, I thought, did a good job of showing some of the irrationalities of objectivism. The few impartial members of the audience agreed that I did. But every time I mentioned Ayn Rand, Branden, or

Objectivism critically, the objectivists in the audience loudly booed me.

Ayn Rand was in the audience and fidgeted greatly during the debate. At one point, when I said, "Ayn Rand's heroes in her novels, such as Howard Roark and John Galt, are utterly impossible humans — or, rather super-humans. They have no flaws whatever; and are literally out of this world." Ayn Rand became terribly disturbed and jumped up, screaming, "I am not going to listen to this debate!" Nathaniel Branden also jumped up to say that he did not think it ethical or honorable for me to attack a person who was not free to speak for herself, and the audience of Objectivists widely applauded him. Of course, I was not attacking Ms. Rand but, according to the subject of my debate with Branden, I was attacking her *ideas* and her *writings*.

I wanted to publish the recording that was made of this debate but Branden would not agree to do so. I therefore wrote a book, published by Lyle Stuart in 1968, *Is Objectivism a Religion?*, which most readers agree is one of the best books I have ever written. Unfortunately, by the time it was published, Rand and Branden viciously broke up their personal and institutional relationship, greatly defamed each other, and resorted to almost everything against each other except murder. Ms. Rand was especially vindictive and thereby proved, in practice, almost everything I said about her and Objectivism. My book, *Is Objectivism a Religion?* — which has been out of print for many years, but can be obtained in some libraries and second-hand book stores — shows in detail why and how Objectivism is narrow, bigoted, closed-minded, inflexible, unscientific, and although presumably atheistic, actually is Fanatically religious. As many readers have written me since 1968, all devout Objectivists had better be encouraged to read it carefully! I am now in the process of revising it and will show how subsequent events — especially the vitriolic condemnation of Branden by Rand — tend to indicate how accurate the book is.

In sum, Objectivism has many good points; but in the extreme form in which Ayn Rand presented it in her writings, it is often very irrational, did not influence REBT, and had better be subscribed to with much skepticism and caution!

◆ ◆ ◆

November 1999

Is it possible to recover from bad therapy? Can one's intuition be recovered, once lost?

◆

Yes, if you don't blame yourself for being so stupid as to succumb to bad therapy and merely accept yourself as a fallible human who made a mistake in being so gullible. Also, assume that the therapist honestly thought that the therapy was useful for you. He or she may have made a mistake in inflicting you with it but is not damnable for making that error. Then try out a more effective type of therapy — such as Rational Emotive Behavior Therapy (REBT) or Cognitive Behavior Therapy (CBT), which is more likely to help you with your problems.

It is unlikely that your intuition was really lost, but only temporarily side-tracked. With effective therapy it can be recovered.

◆ ◆ ◆ ◆

Self-Esteem, Unconditional Self-Regard, Self-Acceptance

February 1999

Q *Carl Rogers suggested three main variables which are essentials for any success in therapy, I'd like to know, what do you personally think about the importance of empathy, congruence and acceptance as factors in the therapeutic process?*

◆

A The three variables of empathy, congruence, and acceptance are very important for success in therapy. Rational Emotive Behavior Therapy (REBT) particularly emphasizes the therapist's expressing these, as well as teaching clients to unconditionally accept themselves, unconditionally accept other people, and accept the adversities of life that they are unable to change.

Rogers clearly stated that these ingredients of therapy are necessary and sufficient to the therapeutic process, but he was obviously overgeneralizing and being somewhat dogmatic about this. People have great constructive abilities and find many different ways of helping themselves change. Many do so through reading and listening to tapes, by having a harsh and unempathic therapist, by working with a noncongruent therapist, by having a remarkable personal experience, and by other self-help and therapy. I show in *Reason and Emotion in Psychotherapy* that Rogers was on the right track regarding the *importance* but not the *necessity* of empathy, congruence, and acceptance in therapy.

◆ ◆ ◆

February 1998

Q *Is it true that REBT stresses the importance of the therapist demonstrating unconditional positive regard for the patient, while not necessarily approving of the behavior?*

◆

A Yes, REBT goes along with Carl Rogers in stressing unconditional positive regard or unconditional self-acceptance (USA), while also pointing out, as Rogers did not, that it is often best to emphasize the client's self-defeating behavior. But REBT also actively teaches clients the value of unconditionally accepting themselves, even when the therapist and other people do not accept them. Otherwise, if clients accept themselves *because* the therapist accepts them they do so *conditionally* and will not accept themselves *un*conditionally. People rate themselves, their totality, as "good" or "bad" when their traits are effective or non-effective. This gets them into emotional trouble. So they had better be shown concretely *how* to achieve USA by a therapist who also gives UOA to them. But dysfunctional *behavior* is to be evaluated as undesirable and changed.

◆ ◆ ◆

October 1997

Q *What is your view of Nathaniel Branden's emphasis on cultivating self-esteem in therapy? It is obvious that REBT/RBT/CBT etc. downplays self-esteem and focuses on USA. It seems that Branden would say that USA is only one of the components of self-esteem that one needs to cultivate for optimum health, happiness, etc.*

◆

A Branden originally defined self-esteem as self-efficacy —
that is, knowing that you are competent and conditionally
accepting yourself because you have the ability to think
properly and master your life conditions. USA means
unconditional self-acceptance — you accept yourself as a
person who prefers to do well but is highly fallible and
therefore often does poorly and may be disapproved of by
others for doing poorly. So you only make the conditions of
self-acceptance:

1. being human
2. being a unique but not a specially competent human
3. being alive or existent
4. being a very fallible human who will make many
   mistakes and errors.

Better yet, philosophically you can choose to rate or
evaluate what you think, feel, and do, once you have
chosen goals and purposes to follow. But you never have to
give global ratings to your *self*, your *being*, your *essence*, or
your *personhood*.

I don't think that Branden, though he is sometimes
vague in this respect, fully understands unconditional self-
acceptance (USA). He still tends to confuse it with self-
efficacy, which is desirable to have but still does not equal
USA or make you a good person. You are not what you do —
as Alfred Korzybski showed in *Science and Sanity* in 1933.

◆ ◆ ◆

September 2000

Q *I am a psychotherapist in the UK and my question is this: Do you consider the constant obsession with a search for self-esteem to be completely missing the point?*

◆

A Yes, when you have a constant obsession with anything, it usually means that you think that you *absolutely must* have that thing and/ or *must* win some person's approval. Your strong *desire* to achieve some goal or win approval is fine. But when you escalate your preference to a *necessity*, you often become obsessed with it, think that it is *devastating* if you don't have it, and are constantly anxious about failing to achieve what you "must" have.

Self-esteem is usually conditional on your achieving a goal or winning people's approval; and your obsession with gaining it usually means that you will denigrate yourself as a person if you don't have it. But self-denigration, of course, lowers your "self-esteem"! So when you *absolutely must* have it, you lose it — unless, of course, you *perfectly* achieve and *always* win people's approval. Lots of luck!

Instead of striving for *self-esteem*, REBT encourages you to achieve *unconditional self-acceptance* (USA). You gain USA by firmly *deciding* or *choosing* to accept yourself as a person *whether or not* you perform well and *whether or not* significant people approve of you. This can be your wise and *preferable* decision. But if you think that you *absolutely must* achieve unconditional self-acceptance, beware! You will then anxiously obsess about achieving it — and thereby lose it!

◆ ◆ ◆

September 2002

I'm an associate fellow of the Institute and in my
therapeutic practice when I teach the concept of self-
acceptance to my client, I am often asked, "But how do I
accept myself? Can you teach me any methods to accept
myself?" I would like to know your view on this question.
What methods can a therapist recommend to his client to
teach self-acceptance?

◆

Actually, there are several ways in which you can accept
yourself:

1. You can simply *decide* to do so and can then *do* it.
   You are a human with a good degree of choice,
   agency, or "free will." All people have considerable
   choice, and can *decide* to accept or not accept
   themselves. You can therefore just *do* it.
2. You can see, as Alfred Korzybski showed, rating
   yourself *totally* or *in general* is really impossible —
   since you are a very complex person who does many
   "good" and many "bad" things during your lifetime.
   You have tens of thousands of thoughts, feelings, and
   actions. Therefore, if you choose to see yourself as a
   "good person," you would have to *only* and *always* do
   good deeds; and if you see yourself as a "bad person,"
   you would have to *only* and *always* do bad deeds. You
   can, consequently, more accurately see yourself as a
   person who does many "good" and many "bad" acts.
   Although you can evaluate all of your *acts* as good
   (meaning effective) or bad (meaning ineffective), you
   cannot legitimately rate or evaluate your complete
   self as good (meaning effective) or bad (meaning
   ineffective). So you can choose to rate your *different*

doings without rating your *total self* at all. You can then accept yourself with your many "good" and "bad" performances.

3. You can figure out that rating your *self* as "good" will work well by giving you confidence or self-efficacy, while rating yourself as "bad" will frequently lead you to self-defeatism, anxiety, and depression. Therefore, choosing to see your *self* as "good" gives better results than seeing your self as "bad." Though this is inaccurate (as Korzybski noted), it is by far your better, more workable choice.

4. You can take the existential position of Carl Rogers, Martin Buber, Victor Frankl, Paul Tillich, and other thinkers, who hold that all people have existence, life, humanness, and uniqueness and that therefore they are all to be accepted as "good," in spite of the fact that they do a number of "bad" things. This cannot absolutely be proven but it again leads to better results. You can therefore hold that your humanity alone makes you — as well as all other humans — acceptable and "good" *persons*.

5. You can hold the Rational Emotive Behavior Therapy position that if you want to survive and be happy, especially when you reside in a social group, you have to evaluate the "goodness" or effectiveness of many of your *behaviors* but not to rate (your basically unrateable) total *self*, *being*, or *essence*. You thereby choose to live and enjoy without taking on the handicaps that almost inevitably accompany self-rating and self-downing.

6. You can firmly believe in a kindly and forgiving God or Higher Power who thoroughly accepts you no matter how well or badly you perform, and through relying on this kind of deity, come to completely

accept yourself. This form of self-acceptance is not entirely unconditional (since you rely on God), but it borrows self-acceptance from the unconditional acceptance of the deity you choose to believe in.

These are some of the many ways in which you can achieve unconditional self-acceptance. USA means that you accept yourself totally *whether or not* you perform well and *whether or not* significant people approve of you and your actions. By the same kind of thinking, you can also teach yourself unconditional other-acceptance (UOA) and thereby *choose* to accept other people while not liking many of the things they do. Again, you have a choice!

◆ ◆ ◆ ◆

Death and Grief

February 2002

 When working with clients who are grieving, how is REBT used to help them through this process?

◆

 REBT does not consider grieving a serious emotional problem. When you have lost someone you love and who added considerably to your life when living, grieving for that relative, close friend, or business associate can be your natural expression of great loss and your strong sadness as a result of that loss. REBT considers sadness, sorrow, and grief healthy negative emotions, even when they are felt intensely and last for two or three years after a loved one has died. When you feel grief, you steadily think about people you lose, greatly regret their absence, are sorry that you did not spend more time with them while they were living, and are saddened that you cannot see them now or in the future. For a while, you are very much aware of them and relive many intimacies you had with them.

Your grief, then, is natural and normal. You would be unusual and perhaps abnormal if you did no grieving. It tends to decrease after awhile, so that you still remember your loved ones, but are not obsessed with them, nor with the horror of being without them. You particularly remember them on their birthdays, holidays, or on anniversaries of special things you did together. You sometimes may be very sad in going over specific remembrances of them. But the initial shock of losing them, and for a while thinking obsessively about them, passes in a few months or a year or two, and you resume your regular life without preoccupying yourself with your losses. Sometimes, you make new attachments — e.g., acquire a new friend or lover. You still remember your lost ones, but take their death in good stride.

Grief, however, can also be accompanied by depression and then can be obsessive for many years. If it is obsessive-compulsive for a considerable period of time and keeps interfering seriously with the life of the grieving person, it is to be suspected that it may be turning into depression. Grievers who are not depressed, according to REBT theory, are usually telling themselves something like, "It's very sad that I lost my loved ones — sad for me and sad for them. I wish they had lived much longer and had continued to be close to me. But, unfortunately, all humans must die, including me. I need not make myself totally miserable and purposeless without their presence; and even though they cannot enjoy themselves as they once did, nothing can be done about that unfortunate fact. It's very bad that they no

longer exist, but I can still lead a good life — as I am sure
they would want me to do. Now that I have suffered from
this real loss, how can I find other people and things to
enjoy, especially since this will most probably be the one
and only life I'll ever have? I can't make up for the parts of
living that my deceased loved ones have missed but I can at
least considerably enjoy my own limited days."

With strong rational beliefs like these, you can grieve
considerably — but not slip irrationally into depressing
yourself. Depression at the loss of some people you cherish
starts off with similar sensible and practical beliefs, but
self-sabotagingly goes on to include several frequent *musts*
and *awfulizings*. For example:

"My relatives (or friends or associates) *absolutely
shouldn't* have died so soon or so painfully!"

"Because they were good people, harmed no one, and
gave me so much joy, it's unfair that they died. Life
absolutely shouldn't be so unfair!"

"It's not merely bad that they died, but it's *awful*!
Nothing could be worse! And terrible misfortunes like
this, *shouldn't* be allowed to happen!"

"I'm so enormously deprived by their dying, that I *can't
stand* such suffering! I never can be happy *at all* without
them! Life never should be that horrible to me! I'm so
miserable without them that I may even kill myself!"

"Because I loved them so much, I *definitely should* have
helped them to live longer. I never did enough for them
while they were living and that makes me a bad,
worthless person!"

"They *should* have taken better care of themselves then
they did! I hate them for not doing so and making me
needlessly suffer by their premature dying."

"It's so unfair and awful that my loved ones died that it
will be horrible if I die before my time, too! My God!

Suppose I do die soon or before I have fully enjoyed my life? How can I be at all happy knowing that this terrible fate may overtake me? I *absolutely must* not die before I am ready to do so! What an awful thought!"

Shoulding, musturbating, and awfulizing in these ways will turn your strong sorrow and sadness at your loved one's dying — which REBT sees as *healthy* negative feelings — into depression, panic, and rage — which REBT sees as *unhealthy*, disturbed negative feelings. Quite a difference!

REBT helps people deal with normal grief and to refrain from escalating it into depression, panic, and rage by showing them that it can be a healthy and normal reaction to the loss of their loved ones. The great sadness that they feel can actually help them in several ways. For example, it can help them to unashamedly feel what they genuinely feel; to cope with reality when it is very grim; to develop hardiness and high frustration tolerance; to plan for a more fulfilling life while they are still alive; to seek to establish other rewarding relationships. REBT shows grieving people that even the death of their loved ones can have rewards for them — if they refuse to depress, panic, and enrage themselves about it.

With people who do depress, panic, and enrage themselves about the death of close intimates, REBT is famous for showing them that this is a *choice*, not a *necessity*. It teaches them how to discover their self-disturbing musts, shoulds, and demands by using many cognitive, emotional and behavioral methods. It especially shows them how to achieve unconditional self-acceptance (USA), so that they never damn themselves for not treating their lost loved ones better when they were still living. Second, it teaches them unconditional other-acceptance (UOA), so that they do not denigrate their dead friends and relatives when these people foolishly contributed to their own demise. Third, it teaches them unconditional life-acceptance (ULA) or high-frustration tolerance (HFT), so that they do not awfulize about sickness, dying, or death when they are (as they often are) unnecessary, unfair, and exceptionally grim.

With the use of these and many other of its multimodal therapy and counseling techniques, REBT, of course, does not eliminate death or make you happy when your loved ones pass away. But if you use it properly, it leads you to *healthy* feelings of sadness instead of, as is all too commonly the case, *destructive* feelings of depression, panic, and rage.

◆ ◆ ◆

June 1996

Q *I frequently work with adolescents who are grieving the death of loved ones — sometimes other adolescents. How do you integrate empathetic support and REBT with these youngsters without alienating them at the onset?*

◆

A In using Rational Emotive Behavior Therapy (REBT) with grieving adolescents — and also with grieving adults — we first show them that grief for the death of a loved one is a healthy, and not an unhealthy, negative feeling. Grief, or extreme sadness and sorrow over an important loss, is very appropriate and stems from the rational belief, "I miss the deceased person very much. I strongly wish he or she had not died, and am quite sad about my loss and about his or her being deprived of a longer existence." In REBT we empathize with this rational belief and the healthy negative feeling, grief, that goes with it and we support the grieving person and sanction her or his great sorrow.

If, however, the adolescent keeps grieving for a long period of time — say, for well over a year — we suspect that she or he is not merely grieving but is also depressed. If so, we look for the irrational beliefs leading to this depression, which usually are along these lines: "Losing the person I love is so bad that I can't stand it. Bad events like this great loss absolutely should not ever occur! It's awful and terrible — *one-hundred-percent bad* — when they happen! I can't be happy at all without my deceased loved one! I might as well be dead, too!"

If the grieving adolescent has extremely depressing beliefs such as these, we support him or her but still show how exaggerated and irrational these ideas are, and how they can be replaced by the kind of rational ideas mentioned above. We help the adolescent — or the adult — still to grieve for the loved one, but not to be severely depressed about his or her real loss.

◆　◆　◆

December 1998

What is your attitude toward your own death and how can REBT be used to help anyone deal with the consciousness of his or her mortality?

◆

At the age of eighty-five, I am not at all anxious or depressed about my own death, which I assume will probably occur within the next decade or so. Some rational thoughts that I use to fully accept my mortality are:

1. All humans die, including me. So immortality is most unlikely — as also is life after death.
2. I'd greatly prefer to live forever in good health, but I obviously don't *have to* do so.
3. Having a limited existence is highly unfortunate, but not *awful* or *terrible*.
4. I'd better gather my rosebuds while I may, for old time is a-flying.
5. Worrying about death will not postpone it and may accelerate it.
6. The state of being dead includes no pain whatever — and no trials and tribulations!
7. When I die I shall probably have 50 books yet unwritten and many joys unexperienced. Too damned bad!
8. I shall probably not die very painfully but if I see that that is happening, I have arranged to have the plug pulled.

◆ ◆ ◆ ◆

How to Do REBT

November 1998

Q *I am a graduate student in a Group Process class. My partner and I are presenting on REBT and have to co-lead a mock group using this approach. We were wondering if there are "typical" questions a group leader would use to challenge a member's irrational beliefs. I realize much depends on the situation and there are no pat answers but some theories offer specific suggestions and I was hoping you could pass some on to us. Our group will deal with anxiety in various forms: fear of elevators, public speaking, approaching the opposite sex, testing. Thanks for any help you can give us.*

◆

A The main irrational beliefs that accompany emotional disturbance are absolutistic shoulds and musts:

1. "I *absolutely must* do well and win the approval of significant others."
2. "People *must* treat me kindly, considerately, and fairly."
3. "Conditions *must* be easy and enjoyable for me."

These irrational beliefs are disputed and challenged in many ways, including these three:

Realistic and empirical disputing: "Where is the evidence that I absolutely must do well and be socially approved? *Answer:* There is no such evidence, only evidence that it is highly preferable for me to do so.

Logical disputing: Does it follow that, because it is highly desirable for me to do well and be socially approved, proves that therefore I must be? *Answer:* Of course not. Does it follow that because I failed at a task several times I am a complete failure who will always fail at it? *Answer:* Not at all.

Practical disputing: Where will it get me if I insist that I must do well and be socially approved? *Answer:* Probably anxious about failing and depressed about being disapproved. Because of my anxiety and depression I am likely to perform tasks poorly and with less approval.

◆ ◆ ◆

March 1997

Q *In restructuring cognitions, is it possible to make an instantaneous, permanent change, or is the change accomplished in increments? It would seem that a change in one's belief in Santa is instant. What about negative, long-held beliefs about oneself, for example? This topic is often discussed in my group therapy with mentally ill and/or chemically dependent individuals.*

◆

A An instantaneous change can sometimes be made by quickly seeing that you never have to put yourself down for failing at an important goal and/or being rejected by someone who is important to you. But once you suddenly and quickly see this, you had better keep seeing it again and again, and convincing yourself over and over that you are never a worthless *individual* no matter what *mistakes* you make nor what *poor acts* you perform.

If you strongly see this many times and also act against your self-downing feelings — by doing shame-attacking and other REBT risk-taking exercises — you will acquire and retain unconditional self-acceptance (USA). Keep thinking about and working at it and see for yourself!

◆ ◆ ◆

July 1998

Q *Do Rational Emotive Behavior Therapists use role playing in therapy with groups? If so, what types of role playing might be helpful? What other techniques might one use in REBT groups?*

◆

A Rational emotive behavior therapy (REBT) often uses group therapy, as described in the chapter on group therapy in *The Practice of Rational Emotive Behavior Therapy* (Albert Ellis and Windy Dryden). Another of my books, *Rational Emotive Behavior Therapy: A Therapist's Guide* (Albert Ellis and Catharine MacLaren) includes a list of specific exercises suggested for group settings.

One of the main techniques used in REBT group therapy is role playing. One member of the group, for example, role plays a job interviewer and another member role plays the applicant. Then the group critiques how the applicant did with the interview and how he or she could do better. If the one playing the applicant becomes anxious, the role play is temporarily stopped, to discover what irrational beliefs are making him or her anxious. These are then disputed and the role play continues. The role play may be done several times until the main role player gains some interviewing skill and becomes more effective. Various other kinds of role plays are used in REBT group therapy, to help group members gain social skills and to show them how to give up the irrational beliefs that accompany their dysfunctional feelings and behaviors.

◆ ◆ ◆

May 1998

Q 1. *How can REBT be applied in the teaching model?*
2. *Does REBT consider the sex and ethnic background of the client when implementing the disputing intervention? If so, how? If not, why not?*

◆

A 1. REBT can be put in simple teaching form and has been used successfully with children and adolescents, and can also be taught to functionally illiterate adults. It can also be taught to less educated clients if the therapist uses simple language to show them how they largely upset themselves and can be shown how to refuse to do so.

2. REBT considers the sex and ethnic background of all clients and does not interfere with their individual and social goals and values — in fact, REBT shows them how to better achieve these values. It also shows them that when they raise their own goals into absolutistic, grandiose demands and musts, they tend to get into personal and social trouble. Therefore, it indicates how they can change these dysfunctional demands back to strong preferences and thus get more of what they want and less of what they don't want.

◆ ◆ ◆

June 2000

Q *You will be glad to know that your film with "Gloria" is still being utilized in our psychology department. This is the series in which you, Dr. Fritz Perls, and Dr. Carl Rogers each had a session with "Gloria." It is my understanding that you stayed in touch with her after these sessions. My question is: Did "Gloria" resolve her problems with her feelings of inadequacies (self-concept), as it pertained to her relationships with men? I do not wish you to violate patient/doctor confidentiality but it would help to resolve many questions that our class had concerning this series.*

◆

A In answer to your question about Gloria in the film that I did with Fritz Perls and Carl Rogers, *Three Approaches to Psychotherapy:* Gloria did stay in touch with me after our session on the film and did resolve her problems with her feelings of inadequacies as they pertained to her relationship with men. She married and credited me in her letters to me with the ability to relate to a man and to marry one partly as a result of the session I had with her during the film. From this session she saw that she was able to accept herself unconditionally in spite of her inadequacies and that she was quite capable of having a good relationship with another man in spite of her previous divorce.

◆ ◆ ◆

April 2000

Q *I saw a video of the "Gloria" therapy session last year. Are there any aspects of it which you would do differently if you were to take part in a similar exercise to illustrate the REBT approach, with a similar client, in the twenty-first century?*

◆

A In the video I mainly handled Gloria's problem with finding a mate. Today, I would deal with her basic problem of self-downing and would use some emotive-experiential techniques, like rational emotive imagery, and some behavioral methods, like *in vivo* desensitization, to show Gloria that she could always unconditionally accept herself even if she never found the "right" man. Her central problem seemed to be considering *herself* a failure if she failed at important projects and at love relationships. I would try to show her that this is a self-defeating overgeneralization that she commonly makes and that will sabotage her goals and values.

◆ ◆ ◆

April 2002

Q *What is the role of empathy in REBT and Cognitive Behavior Therapy (CBT)?*

◆

A The term *empathy*, as it is commonly used in psychotherapy, has several meanings — and they can differ widely, depending on the type of therapy the practitioner uses. Its original meaning stems from the fact that empathizers are people who have many personal experiences, some of which are similar to those of the clients with whom they empathize. Consequently, therapists use self-knowledge and feelings and project them onto clients in order to understand them better and help them solve their problems. This kind of empathy may be accurate and useful, but it may also be misleading and harmful, because empathizing therapists may wrongly conclude that clients feel exactly the way they themselves do and may easily be mistaken about this "fact."

As used in psychotherapy, and especially in Rational Emotive Behavior Therapy (REBT) and in Cognitive Behavior Therapy (CBT), therapists empathize with their clients in several ways:

1. They listen carefully to their clients' narratives and experiences and do their best to understand and feel close to what these clients think and feel.

2. Along with having empathy for clients, therapists also have a considerable degree of sympathy and caring. Supposedly, they chose to become therapists because they enjoy *helping* clients who are in trouble. So they use their general knowledge of people, as well as their knowledge and feelings about themselves, to determine what most distresses their clients and how they, their therapists, can best help them with their problems.

3. REBT and CBT practitioners particularly empathize with the desires, values, and beliefs that their clients are consciously and unconsciously holding. Thus, they try to discover each client's general and personal goals and purposes, and how he or she is thinking, feeling, and behaving to block achievement of her or his own aims.

4. REBT and CBT counselors assume that their clients do not merely *get disturbed* by external events in their lives but that they also partly *disturb themselves* by holding dysfunctional thoughts and feelings *about* these events. So these therapists empathize with their clients by imagining what they themselves (or practically any person) would think and feel if they were upsetting themselves like the disturbed clients are doing.

5. REBT and CBT counselors *guess*, on the basis of their own psychological and personal knowledge and experiences, what philosophies and feelings *lay behind* their clients' dysfunctioning. They empathically *imagine* what these upsetting beliefs and emotions are, and then present their hypotheses to the clients, to see if they agree with them.

6. If their clients *agree* that they subscribe to destructive ideas, feelings, and actions that significantly contribute to their disturbances, the REBT and CBT

therapists show them several cognitive, emotive, and behavioral techniques of *disputing* and *changing* their distress. Then the therapists keep collaborating with their clients to work on plans and activities that will help them become significantly less disturbed.

7. REBT and CBT counselors, as I just indicated, are empathic in several important ways. They empathize with their clients' past and present experiences and feelings. But, more importantly, on the basis of the therapists' *own* general and personal knowledge, they empathize with the core values and philosophies with which clients probably *create* their disturbances. They also sympathetically *care* for their clients and use all their general and personal resources to help them improve their environmentally instigated and self-constructed malfunctioning.

8. Beyond empathy, of course REBT and CBT therapists employ many procedures to help their clients explore their thoughts, feelings, and behaviors, to dispute and change the irrational beliefs that cause their distress, and to bring about other healthy changes in their lives. In short, REBT and CBT therapists are *empathic,* and they are *active* in helping their distressed clients to live happier, more fulfilled lives.

◆ ◆ ◆ ◆

Special Populations

February 1997

Has the Institute made any statement about REBT and diversity? There are those who argue that we need to take diversity into account when we do therapy. That has not been my impression, at least when working with African Americans, Hispanics or women.

◆

A Yes, REBT definitely takes into account several kinds of diversity. People are individuals and are reared in many different kinds of families, cultures, religions, and other environments. They also have unique biological tendencies and proclivities. Although REBT holds that disturbed individuals — or, rather people with such disturbances as depression, anxiety, and rage — usually partially create them with some kinds of absolutistic *shoulds, oughts,* and *musts,* their dogmatic demands are often quite diverse. Thus, one family member may greatly enjoy the taste of alcohol and another may hate it. One client's musts may primarily be related to achievement, another's to being loved, another's to binging on sweets, etc. Clients are also radically different in what kinds of cognitive, emotive, and behavioral methods will best help them change their self-defeating *demands* and *commands* to healthy *preferences.* REBT practitioners, therefore, take considerable trouble to assess the problems of each individual client, to experimentally discover his or her clinical history and reactions to therapy, to try a number of REBT methods to see which ones will likely help this particular person, and to change tactics considerably if certain ones do not work well. Because clients are so diverse, REBT is always multimodal and is designed to follow a consistent theory but to vary its application in many individualistic and multicultural ways.

◆ ◆ ◆

November 1996

Q *I am a first year graduate student, and recently had an opportunity to view your classic session with "Gloria." As I watched, I wondered how your REBT would work with adolescents. What research has been done regarding the use of REBT with adolescents? Do you suggest any modifications of your techniques when treating adolescents? I am very interested in this type of therapy. I plan to work with adolescent patients. I hope you can answer my questions.*

◆

A Considerable research has been done on Rational Emotive Behavior Therapy and Cognitive-Behavior Therapy with adolescents. Some of it is summarized in D. Hajzler and M.E. Bernard's (1991) "Review of Rational-emotive Studies" in *School Psychology Quarterly,* 6 (1), 27-49.

A good deal of material on the use of REBT with adolescents is included in the following books and videos: *Thinking, Feeling, Behaving* by Ann Vernon, and my book with Jerry Wilde, *Case Studies in REBT with Children and Adolescents.*

◆ ◆ ◆

August 1997

Q *Some adolescents have intense lack of trust in adults, society and authority figures. This may be intensified by negative experiences and repeated failures in education as well as personal relationships. As an educator, after establishing a trust bond between adult and young person, what next step would be best — attaining an avenue for*

success through talent development or focus on
restructuring self-defeating concepts?

◆

A Usually, it would be better to focus on restructuring self-defeating concepts, because they would interfere with gaining success through talent development and/or would tend to make adolescents (or adults) disturbed and miserable in spite of their success. However, self-efficacy is an important part of human functioning, and a great many adolescents would not work at achieving *unconditional* self-acceptance but would only let themselves gain *conditional* self-acceptance, contingent on seeing themselves as efficacious. Ideally, they could be taught to unconditionally accept themselves even when they have little talent development, *and also* develop their talents — not to prove they are "worthwhile" but mainly to enjoy and fulfill themselves.

So they preferably should be taught to achieve success through talent development and to honor themselves as worthy humans whether or not they are successful. *Both/and* rather than *either/or* is the best answer to the question.

◆ ◆ ◆

April 1997

Q *My question is about those clients who have a history of child or early adult abuse. I have not found anything in your printed work that may help me work with these clients. Perhaps you can suggest something that I can refer to that may help me identify some irrational beliefs (IBs) and consequences more easily.*

◆

A A history of child or early adult abuse often encourages the client to have the rational beliefs (RBs) that this abuse was very unfair and immoral and that it preferably should not have occurred. In REBT we would encourage clients to retain these beliefs and therefore feel exceptionally displeased, sad, and frustrated about the abuse and its unfortunate effects. Some clients, however, also have the irrational beliefs (IBs) that because the abuse was so unfair and immoral it absolutely should not have occurred, it was therefore totally bad, that the abuser was a completely rotten person, and that they themselves (the abused individuals) absolutely should have prevented the abuse and are worthless individuals because they did not prevent it. Using REBT, we help the clients modify these self-defeating irrational beliefs (IBs) and thereby to reduce their present disturbances — such as feelings of overpowering rage and guilt about the abuse. We also work with these clients to reduce their own possible low frustration tolerance (LFT), so that they are not as likely to abuse their own children.

◆ ◆ ◆

October 1998

Q *Can Cognitive Therapy be used to treat women who are in abusive relationships?*

◆

A Cognitive Therapy (CT) and Rational Emotive Behavior Therapy (REBT) can be used to treat women who are in abusive relationships in a good many ways. For example, many abused women think and feel that they must stay in abusive relationships — and can be shown that they may

choose to stay but they practically never have to do so.
Many believe that they are worthless and that they deserve
the abuse they are getting — which, of course, is nonsense.
Many irrationally believe that standing up to their mates
and insisting that the abuse stop is much too difficult —
instead of believing more rationally that staying with the
abuse is much harder than confronting the abuser and
perhaps leaving him.

Irrational cognitions often follow from and help
prolong or exacerbate relationship abuse. These can be
discovered by REBT and actively disputed and ripped up by
using a combination of cognitive, emotive, and behavioral
methods that are always included in Rational Emotive
Behavior Therapy.

Relationship abusers can also be treated with REBT and
sometimes shown how to be less abusive. Often, however,
they are unreachable and therefore women in abusive
relationships can be successfully treated to confront the
abuser and to get him to stop his abuse, or else be helped to
end the relationship.

◆ ◆ ◆

September 1997

Q *We mental health care workers in the United States
Correctional System have the ability to utilize several
methods of intervention with inmates confined in our
institutions. Many assessments are conducted and many
types of therapies are utilized. How effective is REBT in this
type of environment and do you offer any training,
coursework or text in this particular area of interest?*

◆

A   According to several therapists who use REBT in the correctional system, it is distinctly more effective than other kinds of therapies that are used with prisoners. Few controlled studies have been done, however, to substantiate this clinical finding; and I cannot, at the moment, refer you to any of them. I get quite a few letters from inmates who have learned to use REBT in prison and who tell me that it has greatly helped them. Some of them have, with or without therapy, been particularly helped by reading REBT books, such as my books, *A Guide to Rational Living, How to Control Your Anxiety Before It Controls You,* and *The Albert Ellis Reader.* They say that they have profoundly changed their thinking, feeling, and behavior by reading this material — as far as I can see, they really have done so. As a result of their REBT reading, several of them are studying psychology in prison and hope, eventually, to become counselors and therapists. Let us hope that they do so and are able to work effectively with other prisoners!

◆ ◆ ◆

October 1999

Q   *Attention Deficit Disorder, ADD, is covered by the Americans with Disabilities Act. College students diagnosed with ADD, at some schools, are now able to get more time than non-ADD students to take tests and to do homework assignments. Do you think that this special academic treatment is necessary or a good idea? What is your view on ADD? Has REBT been effective in treating ADD? What studies have shown the effectiveness of REBT on ADD? What are some good resources on the subject of using REBT to treat ADD?*

◆

A It is probably a good idea to give college students with ADD more time to do their homework since, when it is properly diagnosed, ADD is a real handicap that includes physiological factors. Rational Emotive Behavior Therapy (REBT) and other forms of psychotherapy do not directly treat ADD; but REBT treats the anxiety, depression, and low frustration tolerance which frequently accompany ADD and the handicaps that go with it. If people who have ADD go for REBT and other forms of cognitive behavior therapy (CBT) they will avoid putting themselves down for having it, and will therefore deal with its problems much better. They will also be better at coping with the medication which is sometimes useful for ADD, as well as at taking the remedial educational training which is also sometimes helpful in improving the learning inefficiencies that go with ADD. My book, *How to Control Your Anxiety Before It Controls You* — although it doesn't deal directly with ADD — offers help with the kinds of anxiety that often accompany it.

◆ ◆ ◆

May 1996

Q *When you have clients who display intense emotions, do you help them to manage their emotions by zeroing in on their thoughts, or do you initially use another technique?*

◆

A I first help such emotional clients zero in on their thoughts to see what they told themselves to create their intense emotions — paying particular attention to their feelings of anxiety, depression, or rage. We quickly find these thoughts — which are demands and musts on themselves, on others or on external conditions — and we use Rational Emotive Behavior Therapy (REBT) to dispute them and change them into realistic preferences. As the clients focus on the disturbing thoughts that lie behind their disruptive feelings, they almost immediately distract themselves from their demands and temporarily calm down. Then, as they dispute their musts and change them to preferences, the main basis for their disturbed feelings dissolves and they end up with healthy and functional negative feelings of sorrow, regret, frustration and annoyance when unfortunate events occur in their lives. These may still be quite strong, but they are not disruptive.

◆ ◆ ◆

April 1996

Q *How does REBT respond to those who adhere to a biochemical model of mental illness (especially bipolar disorder and chemical dependence)?*

◆

A REBT fully accepts the fact that several forms of mental illness— such as bipolar disorder — are at least partly created by a chemical imbalance. Therefore, REBT therapists frequently help people with such disorders to try lithium, anti-depressants, or other medication after they have been evaluated by a psychiatrist who specializes in psychopharmacology. People with reactive depression and anxiety who at first are not greatly helped by REBT also sometimes can benefit from psychotropic medication, and therefore can use it — under psychiatric supervision — to see if it works without serious ill side effects.

◆ ◆ ◆

June 1999

Q *In REBT terms, how do you explain motives behind the April 1999 Columbine High School shootings and the "copycat" threats, going on? How would REBT be applied as an intervention?*

◆

A There is no single explanation for the Columbine High School shootings. Youngsters who do such shootings and who make copycat threats often suffer from severe personality disorders, which have biological origins and are also exacerbated by social learning. Some main social factors which REBT could work on include:

1. The demand for high social status encourages some youngsters to have to do special dramatic things in order to gain it.
2. Those who have low status are especially motivated to gain higher status by doing something *special.*
3. Those with low status hate themselves and often hate other youngsters with higher status.
4. Almost all youngsters rate *themselves*, and not merely their *performances*, when they do poorly and thereby make themselves feel both worthless and depressed, but also very angry at the system which helps give them feelings of worthlessness.
5. Some youngsters feel so low that they are suicidal but want to kill others as well as themselves.
6. Youngsters who are blocked from getting what they really want often have low frustration tolerance (LFT), demand that they *absolutely must not* be

frustrated, and will do practically anything to relieve their frustration. For these and other reasons, disturbed youngsters may resort to violence.

REBT would first try to get these youngsters, before they were too disturbed, to follow its three major philosophies that prevent their becoming self-hating, hostile, and intolerant of frustration:

1. Unconditional self-acceptance (USA) — accepting themselves whether or not they are performing well or have approval and status with others.
2. Unconditional other-acceptance (UOA) — accepting other people whether or not they behave well, accepting the sinner but not their sins.
3. Accepting the world and its real frustrations and not demanding that these not exist when, unfortunately, they do exist.

REBT uses many cognitive, emotive, and behavioral methods of helping people achieve these three accepting attitudes and thereby undermines disturbance before it becomes serious. When this does not work well enough with individuals with severe personality disorders, then REBT uses its multimodal methods to help them become significantly less disturbed and hence less self-hating and violent.

◆ ◆ ◆

March 1998

◊ *Can Christians benefit from REBT? Can REBT be useful with people who have absolutistic beliefs as revealed in the Bible? Are the absolute standards declared in scripture at odds with rational thinking?*

◆

A Yes, Christians can benefit from REBT. I have a book, with Stevan Nielsen and Brad Johnson, two psychologists who use REBT with Christians and who get some excellent results. The book, *Counseling and Psychotherapy with Religious Persons: A Rational Emotive Behavior Therapy Approach,* shows that the Christian philosophies, particularly that of accepting the sinner and not the sin, often are similar to REBT philosophies of unconditional self-acceptance (USA), unconditional other-acceptance (UOA), and high frustration tolerance (HFT). Christians who believe in a kindly, forgiving God can particularly benefit from REBT.

◆ ◆ ◆

August 1999

Q What are your views about a therapist getting romantically involved with a client? Have you ever done so yourself?

◆

A It is quite dangerous for therapists to get romantically involved with a client, particularly, if they are obsessively-compulsively in love with the client. They then tend to be prejudiced in their observations of the client, and may see him/her in too good or too bad a light. They are not really relating to the client for his/her sake, but frequently for their own interests. If their romantic relationship ends, they may leave the client seriously stranded, without a suitable therapist. They may easily exploit the client for their own sake.

There are many other reasons why therapists definitely should not get romantically involved with their clients and the rules of ethics of the American Psychological Association, the American Association for Marriage and Family Therapy, and the American Counseling Association, among others, clearly oppose any relationship of this sort.

Although I have been attracted to some of my clients, and might have considered them as possible partners if I had not been their therapist, I have never been romantically involved with one, and I shall make sure that I never will be.

◆ ◆ ◆ ◆

Bibliography

Bibliography

Alberti, R. and Emmons, M. (2001). *Your Perfect Right: Assertiveness and Equality in Your Life and Relationships* (8th Ed.). Atascadero, CA: Impact Publishers.

Beck, A. (1976). *Cognitive Therapy and the Emotional Disorder.* New York: International Universities Press.

Benson, H. (1976). *Relaxation Response.* New York: Avon.

Borchert, B. (1996). *Head Over Heart In Love: 25 Guides to Rational Passion.* Sarasota, FL: Professional Resource Press.

Broder, M. (2002). *Can Your Relationship Be Saved? How to Know Whether to Stay or Go.* Atascadero, CA: Impact Publishers.

Burns, D. (1989). *Feeling Good: The New Mood Therapy.* New York: Morrow.

Edelstein, M. and Steele, D. (1997). *Three Minute Therapy: Change Your Thinking, Change Your Life.* Lakewood, CO: Glenbridge Pub.

Ellis, A. (1958). "Rational Psychotherapy." *Journal of General Psychology,* 59, 35-39.

Ellis, A. (1994). *Reason and Emotion in Psychotherapy.* New York: Kensington Publishers.

Ellis, A. (2001). *Overcoming Destructive Beliefs, Feelings, and Behaviors.* Amherst, New York: Prometheus Books.

Ellis, A. (2002). *Overcoming Resistance: A Rational Emotive Behavior Therapy Integrative Approach.* New York: Springer Publishing Company.

Ellis, A. and Harper, R. (1961). *Guide to Rational Living.* Englewood Cliffs, NJ: Prentice-Hall.

Ellis, A. and Knaus, W. (1977). *Overcoming Procrastination.* New York: New American Library.

Ellis, A. and Tafrate, R. (1997). *How to Control Your Anger Before It Controls You.* Secaucus, NJ: Carol Publishing Group.

Ellis, A. (1996). *Better, Deeper and More Enduring Brief Therapy: The Rational Emotive Behavior Therapy Approach.* New York: Brunner/Mazel Publishers.

Ellis, A. (1998). *How to Control Your Anxiety Before It Controls You.* New York: Kensington Publishers.

Ellis, A. (1999). *How to Make Yourself Happy and Remarkably Less Disturbable.* Atascadero, CA: Impact Publishers.

Ellis, A. and Velten, E. (1998). *Optimal Aging: Getting Over Getting Older.* Open Court Publishing Company.

Ellis, A. and Crawford, T. (2000). *Making Intimate Connections: Seven Guidelines for Great Relationships and Better Communication.* Atascadero, CA: Impact Publishers.

Ellis, A. and Harper, R. (2001). *Dating, Mating, and Relating.* New York: Citadel Press.

Ellis, A. and Dryden, W. (1997). *The Practice of Rational Emotive Behavior Therapy.* New York: Springer Publishing Company.

Ellis, A. and MacLaren, C. (1998). *Rational Emotive Behavior Therapy: A Therapist's Guide.* Atascadero, CA: Impact Publishers.

Ellis, A. and Wilde, J. (2001). *Case Studies in REBT with Children and Adolescents.* New York: Prentice Hall Press.

Ellis, A. and Blau, S. (1998). *The Albert Ellis Reader: A Guide to Well-Being Using Rational Emotive Behavior Therapy.* New York: Carol Publishing Group.

Ellis, A. (2001). *Feeling Better, Getting Better, Staying Better: Profound Self-Help Therapy for Your Emotions.* Atascadero, CA: Impact Publishers.

Ellis, A., Nielsen, S., and Johnson, B. (2001). *Counseling and Psychotherapy with Religious Persons.* Lawrence Erlbaum Assoc., Inc.

Hauck, P. (1984). *The Three Faces of Love.* Westminster: John Knox Press.

Hayes, S., Strosahl, H., and Wilson, K. (1999). *Acceptance and Commitment Therapy.* New York: Guilford.

Korzybski, A. (1933/1901). *Science and Sanity.* Concord, CA: International Society for General Semantics.

His Holiness, the Dalai Lama and Cutler, H. (1998). *The Art of Happiness: A Handbook for Living.* New York: Putnam Publishing Group.

Mahoney, M. (1991). *Human Change Processes*. New York: Basic Books.

Pietsch, W. (1993). *The Serenity Prayer*. San Francisco: Harper San Francisco.

Rogers, C. (1961). *On Becoming a Person*. Boston: Houghton-Mifflin.

Seligman, M. (1998). *Learned Optimism*. New York: Pocket Books.

Tillich, P. (1953). *The Courage To Be*. Cambridge, MA: Harvard.

Vernon, A. (1989). *Thinking, Feeling, Behaving: An Emotional Education Curriculum for Adolescents Grades 7-12*. Champaign, IL: Research Press.

Index

A

"ABC" (Activating event-Belief-Consequences) structure, 5, 29-30
absolutist thinking, 29, 37, 84
abuse
client with history of, 120-122
forgiveness and, 44
self-esteem and, 19
sexual, 42
women in abusive relationships, 121-122
acceptance, self. *See* self-acceptance
ADD (Attention Deficit Disorder), 123-124
addictions, 58
adolescents
Columbine High School shootings, 126-127
grieving, 107
REBT's application to, 119
USA in, 120
adversity, REBT's approach to, 6-7
Albert Ellis Institute, 93
Alberti, Robert, 52
alcoholics, co-dependency and, 69
Alcoholics Anonymous, 35
Alder, Alfred, 83
American Association for Marriage and Family Therapy, 129
American Counseling Association, 129
American Psychological Association, 6, 129
Americans with Disabilities Act, 123
anger, 49, 50
antidepressants, 58-62
anxiety, 52-53

approval, of others, seeking, 23
Art and Science of Rational Eating (Ellis), 55
Attention Deficit Disorder (ADD), 123-124
audio-visual materials, use in teaching REBT methods, 9
awakening with anxiety, 53
awfulizing, 38, 40, 105

B

bad therapy, recovering from, 96
behaviors
clinging to the past, 28
distinguishing from persons, 15-16
dysfunctional. *See* dysfunctional behaviors
evaluating your own, 17
irrational. *See* irrational beliefs, behaviors
self-defeating, 27
beliefs
in "ABC" structure, 5, 29-30
about death, 64
about God, 58
about past events, 28
irrational. *See* irrational beliefs, behaviors
life after death, 58
self-defeating. *See* self-defeating beliefs
self-helping, 44
in your own goodness, 16
Benson, Herbert, 24
Bernard, M.E., 119

MORE BOOKS WITH *IMPACT*

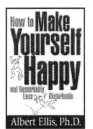

More Books with Impact

Master Your Panic and Take Back Your Life!
Twelve Treatment Sessions to Overcome High Anxiety (2nd Edition)
Denise F. Beckfield, Ph.D.
Softcover: $15.95   304 pages
Help for the 24 million adult Americans who suffer from high anxiety. Proven, research-based methods in a comprehensive anxiety treatment program.

The Assertive Woman (4th Edition)
Stanlee Phelps, M.S.W. and Nancy K. Austin, M.B.A.
Softcover: $15.95   256 pages
Over 400,000 copies sold, the original assertiveness book for women. Already one of the most powerful self-help books ever, this fourth edition is completely revised and up-to-date.

Your Perfect Right: Assertiveness and Equality in Your Life and Relationships (8th Edition)
Robert E. Alberti, Ph.D., and Michael L. Emmons, Ph.D.
Softcover: $15.95   Hardcover: $21.95   256 pages
Eighth edition of the assertiveness book most recommended by psychologists — fifth most recommended among all self-help books! Helps readers step-by-step to develop more effective self-expression.

Feeling Better, Getting Better, Staying Better
Profound Self-Help Therapy for Your Emotions
Albert Ellis, Ph.D.
Softcover: $15.95   272 pages
Healthy thinking, healthy emotions, and healthy behavior are explained, with detailed examples and procedures for building lasting emotional well-being.

Ask your local or online bookseller, or call 1-800-246-7228 to order direct.
Prices effective May 1, 2003, and subject to change without notice.
Impact 〰 Publishers®
POST OFFICE BOX 6016, ATASCADERO, CALIFORNIA 93423-6016
Phone 805-466-5917 • Fax 805-466-5919
e-mail: info@impactpublishers.com • Web at www.impactpublishers.com

Since 1970 — Psychology You Can Use, from Professionals You Can Trust